GOOD
SCHOOLS

H. P. Schoenheimer
Senior Lecturer in Education, La Trobe University Melbourne

Reprinted by permission of The National Press Pty. Ltd., Melbourne

Behavioral Publications   **1972**   **New York**

Library of Congress Catalog Card Number   72-81103
Standard Book Number Paper 87705-025-2
                    Cloth 87705-073-2
Copyright © 1972   Henry Schoenheimer

BEHAVIORAL PUBLICATIONS, 2852 Broadway—Morningside Heights,
New York, New York 10025

Printed in the United States of America

Contents

Author's Note

For those who do not read prefaces — though they should — I have included a Midword within the text.

For those who would like to know, briefly, what this book is about, I should explain that it contains seventeen thumb-nail sketches of schools in Europe, U.S.A., Asia, U.K. and Australia as they appeared to the eye of a professional educator and journalist while he was in orbit.

Most of my life is devoted to campaigning for better education; as I interpret it, that means education that expresses the joy of learning. By definition — my definition — that in turn means education in schools that are based first and foremost on joyful relationships between learner and teacher.

The schools of which I have written here exemplify in their varying and vital ways that concern for the child and the faith in the child without which good education cannot be, and given which it cannot fail. To those who say "It cannot be done" the answer is simple: it is being done. Increasingly affluent nations can turn the will for better education into the deed — if they really have the will. And if they have not, if the teachers who represent — who **are** — the nation within the school have not, then no computerized courses or mass-media instructional devices, however valuable in their minor place, can long disguise the fact.

The old-fashioned, drab "sit-stillery" of a classroom is going out. Like most of the lower forms of life, it dies hard. The new school will be a beautiful place of vital, active and happy learning, its teachers judged by their capacity to make it so, its students by their self-responsible co-operation in discovery, insight and creativity. Nobody who reads this book and then fails to do something to achieve such schools can claim to care about good education. Probably he went to a bad school in the first place.

HENRY P. SCHOENHEIMER

December, 1969

1 I, too, will something make

Tamagawa Gakuen. Japan

From Shinjuku in Tokyo the electric train clatters noisily out in forty minutes to Tamagawa station, passing on its way hundreds of tiny wooden boxes, eight feet from the rarely-silent railway lines, that are homes for some of the sprawling metropolis's teeming millions. And Tamagawa station is named for Tamagawa Gakuen, Dr. Obara's kindergarten-to-university-postgraduate educational village, set, wide and spacious, on 400 acres of tree-covered, hill-and-valley Rousseau country in Tokyo metropolis and in Kanagawa Prefecture.

I have met no greater man anywhere than Kuniyoshi Obara. When he discusses education his eyes flash, his face is alight with animation, his deep voice is vibrant with enthusiasm. In the presence of an English-speaker like myself, he frequently by-passes his interpreter as an impediment to full human communication, and moves into very good and vital English until the complexity of his thought drives him back into his native Japanese.

Dr. Obara has written 38 books. He is at work on an 8,000-page eight-volume 100-year history of New Education in Japan, of which his publishing house at Tamagawa will print 5,000 copies, one to be given free to every university in the world. He has completed four volumes of his projected 15-volume history of the world's religions, a series which is to be sold commercially and the profits handed over to one of the underdeveloped countries so that its education system may be put on a firm philosophic basis from the start.

Dr. Obara lives in a wooden, tree-shaded Japanese home in the heart of the campus that he has planned and built over four decades, so that his students may seek him out when they feel the need of advice and guidance. For eleven hours every week he teaches and lectures at all levels of Tamagawa. He has asked me for my private list of the world's important schools so that he may go on a pilgrimage and learn more about education. One of my treasured possessions is a signed photograph of Dr. Obara, his lithe and sinewy torso partially revealed by the falling of his dark monkish robe from the extended left arm that holds aloft a great eight-foot bow. An arrow is about to speed from the taut bowstring. I saw the shaft reach its mark, for the picture is a "still" from a colour film of Tamagawa, made in 1966, when Kuniyoshi Obara was 81.

It is colour that is the most vivid memory of Tamagawa, colour and the work of children's hands. The school buildings are mainly white among the green trees, but from the high ground red and blue roof-tops and deep brown earth are seen patchworked in. There are flower gardens rich with crimsons and whites and yellows, and lush greenhouses; and there are brilliant friezes, riotous rainbows, that line passageways and surmount entrances and doorways. In autumn the leaves turn golden brown and in spring the cherry blossoms wave above Cherry Avenue and cascade to carpet it. Glory be to God for coloured things! And the junior boys have painted the pig-pens in a pink and pale blue and lavender kaleidoscope design of adjacent triangles and rhomboids.

In the art room, colour is rampant. The ceiling is a mosaic of scores of large squares each containing a different multi-coloured geometrical design made by a student of the junior high school. Posters and pictures and free design and rhythmic tone poems of colour line the walls, and a treasure house of kiln-baked pottery decks benches and floors.

"May I give you this — and this — and this," begged Dr. Obara as the time approached for me to depart. And he plied me, one after another, with great, heavy, expensively bound and lavishly illustrated volumes about Tamagawa: Education at Tamagawa Gakuen; The Elementary School at Tamagawa Gakuen; The Junior High School at Tamagawa Gakuen; Plays and Dances of Tamagawa Gakuen; Fine Arts and Crafts of Tamagawa Gakuen; till mounting fears of a monstrous bill for extra air luggage gave way to the certainty of my inability to carry the sheer weight of any more literature, and we bound them all up, knapsack-fashion, along with a fat Japanese scroll of Dr. Obara's handsome brush-manship, (it shows, a foot high, the Japanese character for "Vision"), in a large green-and-brown silk scarf with which I presently departed, like a wandering scholar of old, to make my peace with the airline company.

And the books are ablaze with colour. The colour of their gold-embossed bright red or grained grey or dark blue covers; and the colour of children's art work — huge room-sized murals, the collaboration of many pairs of hands; and, over and over, magnificently lighted and coloured scenes of dance and drama from east and west: Legend of Galileo, and a Rice Planting Dance, and

Maeterlink's Blue Bird, and a Dance Poem of The Trojan Women, and Momotaro, and William Tell.

Children have their own garden plots in Tamagawa; and amid one cluster of beds stands a giant concrete brontosaurus, thirty feet long and ten feet high, on which a team of eight pupils laboured for a year. As you walk about the campus, you are constantly coming across such pieces of stone and cement work: here a horse large enough to ride on, there a small (five-foot) giraffe; a free-form design standing at a doorway. And in the craft building I found the ongoing work of the fifth and sixth graders — large, decorated, ninety-square-foot folding screens made by the girls, and a ten-foot-long metal-bodied car by one of the boys, and go-carts, including a seven-footer by other boys, and an equally large wood-and-metal helicopter by yet another. And by more ten-year-old and eleven-year-old artists life-size figures of archers and swordsmen and bushido warriors done in gilded rope over wooden frames; and a six-foot human figure carved from a great tree-trunk; and weaving, and woodwork, and sculpting from Paris plaster; and Japanese character writing carved (by two boys) from a two-foot-by-five-foot block of wood; and religious tapestries and friezes and a life-size plaster cast; and, discordant note amongst the religious themes, a fearsome, mobile machinegun ingeniously mounted on to a tricycle by three demure and doll-like little girls.

I, too, will something make and joy in the making! The large circular ornamental pond where goldfish glide among the water lilies was made, of reinforced concrete, by pupils of the elementary school with the minimum of adult guidance. The under-twelves mow hay and cultivate cabbages and harvest their grape and monster pumpkin crops and tend the cattle and the bees (Tamagawa is famous for its bees) and changed the rickety old wooden bridge for a concrete one. Older children mend roofs and make roads and do the major work of erecting some of the more simple buildings. In handicraft they progress to bookbinding and stone relief carving, assembling radios and watches, and making violins and pianos. It takes a Tamagawa student a full year to carve a violin by hand, and it takes eight or ten senior boys and girls as long to make a case for a piano and assemble the parts. And you have not understood the spirits of Pestalozzi's *Arbeitsschule* at all if you are surprised to find, along with photographs of these and a hundred other activities, pictures of children cleaning the toilets. There is a proud motto of Tamagawa "Be the first one to take charge of the most unpleasant, the bitterest, the hardest, the most difficult and unprofitable work in life, and do it with a smile."

But this is only one side of Tamagawa Gakuen's activities, the work of the hands; and even that is in unfairly brief summary. For if there is a key to the full story of Tamagawa it is the Whole Man concept of New Education — head, heart and hand;

thought, feeling, action. And over all, Pestalozzi's teaching of *Arbeitsschule*, education by working, creating, experimenting, thinking and performing for oneself.

Outside of Tamagawa, Japanese education is narrow, formal, bookish, thorough and demanding, forcing the student to spend a frightening proportion of his waking time in preparation for the most fiendishly competitive examination system in the world. "The student who sleeps five hours will fail," ran a bitter saw of the hag-ridden adolescent. "He who sleeps four hours will succeed." It is cold hard truth that entry to the most highly regarded kindergartens is by examination. It is only a slight exaggeration — made by Japanese educationists — that failure to gain entry to a prestige kindergarten means the end of one's chance in life: for the prestige kindergarten leads to the prestige elementary school and so on, over the mountain-steep examination barrier, to the prestige university. If absolute, unswerving single-minded application and incredibly intense specialization can be as effective in the field of learning as the Japanese have made them in industry, then a typical Japanese education is patterned to produce the highest scholastic achievement known to man.

And against all this, for half-a-century and more, Kuniyoshi Obara has set his calm saintly face, still the face of a man thirty years his junior. "The students of Tamagawa Gakuen know how to carry manure but can also play the piano," he states. "They can mop floors as well as excel in tea ceremonies; they are able to clean gutters and at the same time sing Beethoven's Ninth Symphony; they can burn charcoal and they can act great drama; they can chop wood as well as paint; and they can calculate on the 'soroban' (abacus) but are equally at home with sacred writings."

There is more, much more than this at Tamagawa. But old man Obara (it is the name given him in a tribute book by a disciple and former student) challenges the examaniacs on their own ground. He does not merely claim that education of the whole man is ethically better than narrow intellectualism. He claims also :hat it is ultimately the most effective route to intellectual attainment. And he points with pride to the performance of his students in the nation-wide junior high school examinations — an average 80% to the national 65%, with many acknowledged good schools cutting out at 72%.

Tamagawa has its own entrance examinations for Junior High School and Senior High School levels. Incoming students can shade Tamagawa's own products in work involving rote memorization; in everything else—inventiveness, understanding of principles, experimentation—they fall behind. It is not, of course, merely a school that is up for judgement: it is two philosophies of life and learning, two views of the nature of the child, two approaches to human fulfilment now and in the future.

Tamagawa Gakuen has a kindergarten with 120 three-to-five-year-olds; a six-year elementary school with 600 pupils; a three-year junior high with 600; a three-year senior high with 1200. Its full-time university enrolment is 5,500, and another 32,000 undergraduates study by correspondence. (By 1968, in the postwar period 150,000 teachers had qualified by means of Tamagawa's external courses and residential summer schools.) Of the 600 students normally in residence, 400 are at the university level.

This is not the story of Tamagawa University. Only a quarter of its students are Tamagawa products, and Dr. Obara finds the rest (who come by government edict) strongly biased towards rote learning. He says that, for most of them, it takes a year of re-education before they can begin to learn. The first university year (fortunately?) is a general year. The study and making of ceramics and the study and performance of dances are part of the course. The faculty of education is large and prestigious, and half of Tamagawa's school teachers are trained there. The Educational Research Unit has some 400 active researchers and draws scholars from abroad for study and conference. In future, by government regulation, it will be necessary to hold a Tamagawa certificate to become principal of an elementary school or a junior high school.

To many people the term "new education" is synonymous with disorder. To others, more sophisticated, it implies a very great measure of freedom. For Dr. Obara, the whole-man concept is central; freedom and self-responsibility go just so far and are part of a larger whole.

The school is a unique blend of Pestalozzi (with a very strong emphasis on Christian religion), a widely European culture reaching out into internationalism, and Japanese traditionalism.

Dr. Obara writes much of education, at a theoretical and philosophical level. Beauty and holiness, creativeness and richness of living are his touchstones, and education of head, heart and hand must promote all of these. He aims to reconcile the harmonious universality of Platonism with Rousseau's spirited defence of the dignity of man.

Fine words, to which many educational systems pay lip-service. What do they mean in practice, here at Tamagawa?

There is, indeed, a lot more of the Locke-Rousseau "hardening" than Western new education has generally emphasized, a reflection of Obara's own youthful experience. For the residential student, who must be at junior high school level or above, day begins with a drum-roll before dawn that summons him to the cleared summit of Seizan (Sacred Mountain) highest point of the school campus.

Summer or winter (and winter means heavy snow) Dr. Obara leads the dawn assembly's morning service.

There is, too, more respect of authority than Western progressives would countenance. The service begins with the raising of the National Flag followed by prayers, songs, and the school specialist's particular version of Danish-style gymnastics.

Breakfast, like all the other meals of the day, begins and ends with songs and prayers, and is eaten to the ru:ning accompaniment of a "diningroom sermon" from Dr. Obara — points of etiquette, moral exhortations, lofty comments on current in-school and out-of-school events.

After breakfast, the boarders study privately until 8.45 a.m., the arrival time of the day students who commute from Tokyo or Kanagawa. For morning assembly (in the open air) a drum and fife band plays the march. Once a week there is a half-hour assembly for prayers and hymn-singing. Nobody may opt out of religious observance: to Dr. Obara, religion is as integral to education as words are.

Class teaching occupies the morning, and after lunch all student time is devoted to music, gymnastics, *arbeit* and free research or self-chosen study. School ends at 3 p.m., but all students stay until 5 p.m. at least once a week for co-curricular activities.

When the day students have left for home, the boarders continue with other forms of *arbeit* such as animal care, library work, building work and the many chores of a school that, on principle, has no janitors.

Songs sung at dinnertime are the world's great classics. After dinner there is study till 9 p.m. and lights out at 9.30. "We feel sorry for the students of other schools who are obliged to study until after midnight preparing for entrance examinations." Granted. But they do not all assemble for dawn service daily.

English begins in first grade. I talked to children as young as ten years — a slow, plodding, careful conversation, with a lot of doubt as to how much was going across. But they laughed when I did, and answered my questions with the aid of their English teacher.

From another lesson, I brought away with me a foolscap-sized "book report sheet", oral recording on one specially-prepared side, written record and illustration on the other. The story is a Chinese legend, and the report, in Japanese, was made by an Indonesian boy who had selected this particular book.

At a higher level I saw twelve-year-olds busy at self-directed science assignments — making drawings and charts from books, making their own microscope slides of fibres and flower sections. This was a "free research" period, but clearly it was also science period as scheduled.

A fourth-grade music lesson was a memorable experience. Tamagawa students are quite sophisticated about visitors of many hues and visages. They turned face about from the blackboard and sang me (and my teacher-guide, I suppose) a short welcome song. Then a slight brown boy came and shook hands with me and conducted a second greeting song. Like the first, it was sung with plenty of vigour and happiness. Then the class went on with its work.

A vital lesson all the way, with rhythm and music **happening** in all the lesson, rather than being talked about. Beating time with clapping, then stamping, then both together, then both along with the piano, then all this plus the singing of the words. The song, they told me, was called "Dancing with the Wind". They sang with ease and poise, their bodies and voices participating in the rhythm, and one after another, at a signal from the teacher, these ten-year-old boys and girls took turns to keep the singing going uninterruptedly by conducting, beating and stamping time and singing in front of the group, one stanza each. They played for me, on their recorders, a couple of simple tunes composed by members of the group, and "When the Saints Go Marching In"; and then it was time to leave, so I marched out in strict tempo, waving to 35 of the happiest classroom musicians I have met.

Music, it should be clear by now, is as fundamental to Tamagawa's activities as art and craft are. When groups of 30 or so Tamagawa students (of any age from 10 to 21) tour Europe, Asia or the Americas, giving displays of dance and drama, they take their own musicians with them. The massed choir and orchestra are vital elements in many of the school's annual occasions.

First event of the year, and highlight of it for boarding students, is the New Year's Day ceremony. At 11.55 p.m. on New Year's Eve a huge bonfire is lighted on Seizan, its flames symbolizing light, colour, heat, strength, beauty, the burning away of sin, and burning hope for the year to come. Midnight is signalled with one hundred and eight drumbeats, followed by prayer and song. Then the students disperse, but before sunrise they have bathed and dressed in their best clothes, and are back on Seizan to watch the white and pink winter dawn break gloriously over the eastern mountains. The National Anthem and the hoisting of the National Flag are followed by the school song and New Year's Day songs and, at 8 o'clock, by the serving of Ozoni (a Japanese rice dish) in Dr. Obara's reception room.

Commencement days in March and April (which is cherry blossom time) are important occasions in all Japanese education. The traditional Japanese Girls' Festival in March, the Boys' Festival in May, and the Tanabata festival (the Festival of the Weaver or Star Vega) on July 7th, are honoured with music and song. October's second Sunday brings a vast massed display of athletics, and gathers Tamagawa alumni from the four corners of Japan. And Christmas is the traditional European season, involving day and boarding students in great four-part choral renditions of "Silent Night" and the old carols, which echo from valley to valley and through the woods. "We consider that education without religion is nothing but a corpse," says Obara.

Within a Japanese setting, Tamagawa's co-education is a daring innovation. The school teaches the lesson of care and concern for others by action — help for a child who is deprived, a deliberate policy of admitting some needy and some physically handicapped children, a gift of a medical microscope to Dr. Schweitzer, aid to poorer villagers as an *arbeit;* but it reinforces the lesson of doing with moralizing lectures whose value the Western world has come to doubt. The scroll that now hangs in my study showing the Japanese character for "Vision" is matched by an etched motto in English on one wall of the school. "No vision — people perish." But the vision that is chiefly praised is the vision of benevolent authority rooted firmly in the past.

I believe the children of Tamagawa enjoy their education, within a framework. That framework represents the Japanese paternalism which reaches back to Emperor worship and flows on into politics, society and industry, where every Japanese worker has a guaranteed job till he retires from the company that acts as father-figure throughout his life. Tamagawa six-year-olds do not call Dr. Obara "Kuniyoshi" or cut lessons when they feel like it. Nor, like Summerhill twelve-year-olds at school with that other grand old man of education, A. S. Neill, do his scholars tell him not to be so bloody silly and ignominiously vote his proposed school rules out of existence. The sexual revolution in British and U.S. universities is in line with Neill's free-and-easy regime for a couple of decades, where adolescents bathed together and Neill publicly deplored that a Puritan electorate prevented him from letting them sleep together. Asked whether co-education is satisfactory, Obara — whose segregated dormitories have a good many hundreds of yards between them — says, "Yes. Of course we must be on guard every minute. Fundamentally it works because of basic training and discipline founded on religion." I should like to be a fly on the wall when Neill and Obara argue.

"Every night before I go to bed," Kuniyoshi Obara assured me, gesturing through the study windows of his hill-set home, "I look down over the dormitories and pray for God's blessing on all my children." He prays sincerely, a devout Christian, born of a Buddhist family and adopted into a Shintoist one, a man who has given his life to the vision splendid as he has seen it.

There are not enough Kuniyoshi Obaras.

2 Three per cent.

Franklin delano Roosevelt School
for the physically handicapped. England

You are in Swiss Cottage, London, watching a film. Not a professional film, a short movie showing a school's Christmas social. Coloured balloons and paper chains, festoons of rainbow lights, holly, glistening tinsel, Christmas bells, multi-hued paper lanterns. A long-haired pop group beats out raucous modern rhythm. Shouts, squeals, laughter, and pink and green and yellow streamers spiralling to landings across the room.

The Franklin delano Roosevelt School for physically handicapped children, is named — as inspiration and tribute — for the greatest cripple the world has known. As the compulsive rhythm thrusts into brain and muscle, twisted, handicapped children struggle from their wheelchairs (to the unutterable delight of their guardian physiotherapists), clutch unhandicapped partners, laugh and chatter and sway to the music.

A pale, quiet, very thin, well-dressed young lady of seventeen sits, unsupported, in a chair at the side of the room, watching, smiling, beating the tempo with one foot, obviously enjoying herself. Except perhaps for her pallor, you are not to know, as the camera focuses closer on her, that she is too weak to stand for more than a few seconds at a time, that she came almost direct from her hospital bed to be here.

Seventeen. In the 1960's. And how would you have organized her education (the principal asked me sotto voce) if you had been responsible for it (as the school had) since she was four?

I pondered the question as the guitar rumbled frenziedly to the player's back-produced near-tune, and the drummer flung back his sweating mop and the organist crashed out thunderous chords to make himself audible. Basic skills of course. Environmental studies. Plenty of art, music, literature to compensate for lack of sport? Careful choice of vocational subjects for employment of the handicapped?

15

"Does it make any difference," went on the principal's soft voice, "if I tell you that she died — quite expectedly — of leukemia two weeks after the social?"

Education is not merely preparation. It is living **here** and **now**, living in and into one's whole environment, and living joyfully. For to speak of anything as education which gives no joy is to demean the word and the child and the educative process. And the twin face of joy is love, and love of the child is the first great and completely indispensable qualification of the true teacher.

Thus it is at Franklin delano Roosevelt School. In a hundred schools in a score of countries I have seen no greater devotion than that of these teachers at FDR.

And yet dedication, social conscience, humanity, courage, untiring zeal — these alone are not enough. True insight — as those at the school well know — comes from the marriage of love and awareness. Teachers of the handicapped must be intellectually alert to the growing wealth of knowledge of new techniques. They must be equipped to cope with situations more difficult and more variable than those faced in any other kind of classroom. What was once regarded as an easy escape for the teacher who could no longer stand the strain of normal classes is coming to be seen as an area demanding the most able educators if its work is to succeed.

Remember as you read on, that every child in this school is one of nature's most cruel errors — a severely handicapped child.

The Inner London Education Authority is amongst the most progressive in the world. In its program for the education of the handicapped it has been far-sighted and generous. Franklin delano Roosevelt School is a product of its policy, a school for 150 physically handicapped children aged from 2 to 18.

The building is graceful, pleasing, even inspirational. Structured on simple lines, it blends warm tones of brick, cool tones of wide expanses of glass, and inside, the richness of polished cedar and mahogany woods. The grounds are green with grass and trees.

Indoors, the problems have been foreseen and solved, functionally and aesthetically, as is the way of all good architecture. The building is all on one level. Floors are specially treated to avoid risks of slipping, there are wide doors and corridors for wheelchairs. Special tables are shaped with cut-out segments so as to admit wheelchairs and to provide support to the seated child, and toilets are specially designed also.

Supporting rails have been erected at strategic points in the ground. But, quite deliberately, subsequent planners have developed an adventure playground with enormous concrete sewerpipes as tunnels for crawling through, and large flower pots as obstacles for speeding wheelchairs to negotiate, and a climbing frame, and a hanging rope with supporting ropes. For the spirit of adventure is challenge.

Who comes to FDR? The truest answer is, "Any child in the area whose handicap is so great that he would be better off there, in terms of his all-round, intellectual, social, emotional and physical development, with special care and provision." It is an answer that depends on careful judgement — for there is value in not separating from normal schooling the child who can manage to fend for himself, as there is also value in educating the more fortunate to deeply felt active sympathy and aid for those who need it.

It is an answer, too, that depends on facilities and finance. Even in Britain, less than one per cent of the school population is in special schools, whereas the best estimates are that at least two and perhaps three per cent of the child population have learning handicaps so severe that the children can be expected to make real progress only if special provision is made for them. Many industrially and socially advanced countries show similar percentages of need.

Camden Town Council health authorities — within whose area the school is situated — keep an "at risk" register of all births where some follow-up is thought necessary; and the medical officer will recommend attendance at Franklin delano Roosevelt where he judges it appropriate. Parents have a right of appeal to the local education authority or to the Department of Education and Science against the decision.

Who comes to FDR? No more polio cases (though a few remain from earlier years) thanks to the medical miracle that has wiped President Roosevelt's affliction from the face of Britain. But children with leukemia and children born with serious heart ailments and children with that terrible condition known as spina bifida — split spine — who in earlier times used to die soon after birth, or develop hydrocephalis (water on the brain) but who now survive as bright youngsters — crippled from the spinal break down.

Who comes to FDR? Cerebral palsied children constitute half the enrolment of the school — boys and girls suffering from a muscular dystrophy which, in the present state of medical science, is progressive: the sufferer's condition must deteriorate: what he is ever going to learn he must learn fast and soon.

Who comes to FDR? Michele comes, second of two children of a middle-class family, she and her sister both under irrevocable sentence of debilitation through muscular dystrophy. The working-class tend to neglect their handicapped, the middle-class suffer intense emotional strain. The mother had sent Sandra, the elder sister, to a boarding institution, unable to bear a life that included her in the home. When Michele also proved to be afflicted she could not surrender her other daughter but lived — disintegrating emotionally — in a state of agonized ambivalence — loving and hating her remaining child. The father, elderly, alcoholic and inadequate, stood by helpless.

At Franklin delano Roosevelt, Michele found love and acceptance and incredible patience. No physiotherapist can cure her physical condition, but her hurricanes of fury are moderating, she is learning better adjustment daily, mother and child depending for sanity and security on the school's help.

Ilona comes to FDR. Cerebral-palsied, dark-haired little daughter of a highly intelligent Hungarian mother, Ilona, at six, is learning to walk and to crawl and climb, all in a meticulous program carried out with infinite solicitude — a program where every inch gained is a minor triumph that clears the way for other inches to come. Her language development is closely linked to her swimming tuition (hydrotherapy is vitally important in the school) and, because she also has some brain damage, she works at her "normal" lessons in a special group.

Ilona's mother, tense and anxious, stayed at the school all day through the child's first two weeks, crying steadily in the physiotherapist's office as the truth dawned on her of the full extent of her daughter's handicap, which she had disguised from herself as late development. Now, having faced the situation, she still comes often, to help her own child and others. Daily she watches as Ilona learns to bear her affliction and yet enjoy a life that showers on her so much warmth and affection and indefatigable understanding.

"When medicine fails," says Stanley Segal, principal of FDR, "only education can help. So frequently, parents say, 'At last we have found a school that offers hope'."

A classroom at Franklin delano Roosevelt is in some ways like and in others unlike a good classroom in any progressive school. There is a profusion of materials for eye and hand. In the infant rooms, easels and scales, paints, boxes of games, books and number blocks; dolls and flowers and a Little Mermaid and pot plants and alphabet charts and magnetized letters to stick on boards and a Wendy House and a zoo chart and pictures, some purchased, some drawn by the children. At higher levels there is a change to bring in clocks and aeroplanes and robots, a calendar, cardboard coins, money tables charts and so on. The upper school adds its maps and globe and science pictures and more sophisticated apparatus.

The children work as individuals, some of them on chairs and at tables, some in wheelchairs at specially designed benches, others, the most afflicted physically, in chairs that have been ingeniously constructed to support weak or deformed little bodies. Some children learn in very much the same way as their more fortunate brethren do. In other cases, hands that are loath to obey and minds that seek to know, but oh, so slowly, grapple with intricacies where the normal child finds no problem.

So the culture is mapped and each learns what he can — of words and things and numbers and the heritage of the past and the skills that undergird modern living.

What of the arts? There is much work with colour, design and picture-making, with groups often working on a combined project, say, a mural of Mexico or a scene, *The Countryside*, that will make a more satisfying display than the less able individuals can manage alone. Needlecrafts and creative crafts merge into handiwork in one direction and domestic subjects in another. Both girls and boys take woodwork and cookery. The woodwork room has the usual complement of vyces, cramps, coping saws and other tools. I saw much brasswork — a kangaroo, a bull's head, a donkey, a lizard — as well as two boys making stools, a girl sandpapering an almost complete cupboard, somebody's part-finished sailing-boat, and so on. I am told that the best and most delicate jobs of cake-icing are frequently the work of boys. For a dramatized version of the "Festival of Lessons and Carols" performed at Christmas, the art classes designed royal robes and costumes.

Drama includes improvisation, mime and playmaking, with casts of 40 and more performing in the round. (Six candidates in a year passed the examinations of the London Academy of Music and Dramatic Art.) Music involves percussion and group singing, much appreciation, and, in conjunction with John Keats School, a choir and small orchestra.

The complex web of interaction that is a single human being links mind and body, intellect and emotion and physical behaviour in bewildering action and reaction and counter-reaction. Grave physical handicaps create psychological ones, psychological problems shade into learning difficulties. Some children have gross perceptual problems. Where most of us see a square, they see four disconnected lines on different parts of the page. Ask them to write a letter D and straight and curved lines appear scattered over the book. For others the handicap is not a perceptual one but a motor one — finger muscles with only the grossest control.

Here are little kiddies of four and five moving themselves round the classroom on stunted limbs, leaning on chairs and noisily shoving them along in the desired direction. Here a boy needs more water for his painting. He cannot get it for himself, the teacher must bring it. Here is a girl of four, badly deformed, whose delight it is to sit, supporting her little body in a "nest" of two old motor-car tyres stuck one on top of the other, until, fatigued after twenty minutes, she must be carried back to her chair. Here two boys in wheelchairs are fighting, very much as unhandicapped children do. They must be firmly but gently parted without being made to feel their helplessness to adult strength. Here is the physiotherapist to take Robyn for her daily hydrotherapy session, so Robyn's work must stop, to start again later.

You gaze at this microcosm of handicapped humanity and at the teacher serenely, smilingly coping with twenty on-going situations (for you can walk unexpectedly into the classroom a dozen times in a day and find the teacher serene and smiling), and you wonder how, as a teacher of other children with no such crosses to bear, you could ever have found it necessary to raise a voice or a hand in anger.

And yet, in a very fundamental sense, the one principle of education is the same: understand the individual. Understand him and care for him.

Children may come to Franklin delano Roosevelt School at any age from 2 onward. Some stay to age 18 or 19. A few may be sufficiently rehabilitated to join an ordinary school. This will usually happen by age 10 or 11 if it is to happen at all, though in odd cases children will go to a College of Further Education or even to an 11+ grammar school. These are the exceptions, however; the majority, if they stay in the area, stay in the school.

On his admission, a child's record will show his medical and social background. If he has previous educational experience there will be a record of this also. If he is younger than six he is likely to begin in the nursery class where the teacher will observe his behaviour to see how appropriate this placement is. If he is older, a number of factors will influence the decision: the needs of the child are paramount, of course, and as some highly sensitive children will respond readily to one kind of personality and reluctantly to another, placement may depend more on this factor than on skill or attainment or the policy of limiting all class groups to a maximum of 20. Promotion is "one at a time at any time", any time, that is, when the child is ready for it.

The teacher learns the case history of every child in her care. She must individualize each work program to meet the individual limitations — and strengths — of each pupil. Her role, indeed, is much more akin to that of the consulting physician than of the mass instructor. She must try to diagnose the social and emotional as well as the intellectual needs and capacities of each child, and try to systematically provide the experiences that the child requires. Unlike the physician, however, whose goals are fairly clearly indicated by the very nature of the human organism, she must set up objectives, as one does with normal children, not as barriers or hurdles or employment qualifications, but as stars to steer by, indicators of the general direction of progress.

Always the organization is geared primarily to the children, only afterwards to scholarship. So, when staff meet once a week to discuss problems, they are the problems of individual children and their adjustment, though, inevitably, the deepening of insight into educational techniques is closely allied. The task is not simple, though in principle it is the same as with every child: how to extend the learner to the full without making demands that pass beyond his limits. We have not learned to perform it well with the normal. How much more difficult here.

Special education is not cheap, either in money or in the man-hours it consumes. In addition to the principal, the school has the services of 8 full-time teachers, 6 half-time ones and a nursing class assistant. There are four full-time and one part-time physiotherapists, four physiotherapy students in the final year of training, one full-time nursing sister. Ten attendants — one to each bus — accompany children to and from school, toilet those who need this attention, accompany children on outside visits, push wheelchairs when necessary. A doctor attends on one morning a week, a psychologist and a psychiatrist each visit regularly and on request. There are part-time teachers for the partially sighted, the partially hearing, and those needing speech therapy; and there are a part-time secretary, schoolkeeper (janitor) and gardener.

I asked about the cost of all this. The principal thought the question misplaced. "By world standards, Britain is still a wealthy country. A nation which can spend scores of millions of pounds every year on cigarettes can afford to buy care and happiness for all its handicapped children." He spoke of those earlier civilizations that have killed their less able members and argued that they have proved to be lacking in those emotional dimensions which are essential for co-operative human relationships and therefore for ultimate survival. A large thesis, not without current relevance. He felt, too, that at each stage we are not merely assisting, but moving the frontiers forward, learning to diagnose for both prevention and treatment. Today mentally handicapped children who would have been shut up in institutions a generation ago can be trained to do useful work. Tomorrow — who knows? On my shelf is a very thin and very simple and very small book. It is called "The Diary of Nigel Hunt". It is written by a mongol — a feat as unthinkable twenty years ago as organ transplants, one made possible by a lifetime of parental devotion and courage.

Does the severely physically handicapped child become a fully functioning citizen? Journalist-like, I wanted some outstanding and triumphant case histories for my book — the crippled boy who became a university lecturer, perhaps, or the armless girl whose brilliant mouth paintings were hung in the Tate. Again Segal insisted that my values were wrong: I must measure in terms of happy, confident human beings, and whether that happiness and confidence came to them as academics or artists or as typists or packers in a warehouse was surely a very secondary consideration, once one abandoned the inbuilt prejudices of a competitive, middle-class outlook.

"If you want statistics," he went on, "about a third of these children will acquire the capacity to enter the working world — though few if any at a very high level. Perhaps another third will be in sheltered work, having reached the same standards but needing more support; and a further group will be unable to work. A very small proportion will go on to Further Education. I hope all of them will live, but I cannot forget the probability that some of them will die. Our task here is to make life more endurable and enjoyable, to try to develop the kind of character that will enable them to see the stars rather than the dust."

The notice boards in the foyer of FDR greet you joyously with beautiful, intricate, delicate paintings that give no indication, other than the small printed captions beneath, that they were painted with brushes held in the mouths and the feet of those whose hands were not at the artist's command. There are great, glowing travel posters above a list of school visits — to the Tower of London, the Planetarium, the Science Museum, the Telephone Exchange, the Airport, the Opera House, the Tate Gallery, the Geological Museum, the Royal Mews, the Museum, Lords Cricket Ground — all for one small school of 130 severely handicapped children. And all for the month of May. At vacation times journeys take the children to Kent and Cornwall and to the Continent.

FDR participates in the Special Schools' Annual Sports Day, which includes snooker and table-tennis, javelin (distance and precision), discus, medicine ball, volley ball, wheelchair football, walk relay racing, obstacle racing, five-a-side football, wheelchair slalom, and swimming races up to 100 yards.

Archery has been introduced by the physiotherapists as an evening club activity, along with table tennis, drama, art, craft, music and swimming.

The school has a youth club, Scout Group, Cub Pack. The School Council consists of ten pupils elected by students and staff, plus four co-opted members. It discusses and guides work for the Save the Children Fund (there is something especially heart-warming in this), the school tuckshop, school uniforms, school outings and school socials.

Head of the school council are the Mayor and Mayoress. I was present on the day of official installation. A meeting of the full school in the hall was attended by the Lady Mayoress of Camden Town who placed the robe and chain of office on Maureen, the school's mayoress for the year, and Maureen made a little speech of thanks. Philip, the newly-elected mayor, spoke by tape recorder of his hope of fulfilling his duty of assisting to run the school so that everybody in it, students and staff, should enjoy life to the full. It was somehow symbolic that Philip was in hospital to have the plaster cast removed from one leg.

Parents, too, attended the ceremony. Often, parents need as much support from the school as do their children. Helping the child, and coming to understand how he is helped, is one way of being supported. So when a child is admitted, parents visit and talk to the principal and to the doctor and the class teacher and the physiotherapist. They are invited to visit the classroom whenever they please and to stay as long as they wish — indefinitely, if they desire. Apart from fundraising, the Parents and Friends Association meets to discuss mutual problems: the jealousy of a brother or sister who feels that the handicapped one is getting more than a fair share of parental love and attention; the too-common, almost superstitious avoidance, by peers of the normal child, of a home which has a physically handicapped boy or girl in it; and the terrible drain on sheer energy and emotional strength of meeting the physical and psychological demands that come from the soul of the permanently afflicted. (The school is trying to build a child-minding service for self-help.)

"Put it all together for me," I urged Stanley Segal. "What is your purpose here in Franklin delano Roosevelt?" And as he spoke, I made notes.

"I am here as part of a community which is seeking to make our society a little more humane. I see this school as part of the work going on nationally and internationally towards recognizing individual rights and changing people's attitudes towards each other, not least towards the most handicapped of our population.

"To me the world is a single country and, in principle, a single race. I am sure of one thing, whatever else I am unsure of: quite often one has ideals that lead to activities which create situations the very reverse of those intended. Here, as far as is humanly possible, one is certain of what one is doing. It can only be good to help those who are handicapped to recognize and develop their strengths. It can only do good to push down the walls of the school so that the outside world can come in, and so that the children inside can be taken out to extend their experience and become adjustable to the demands of the community.

"I think, too, that it can only do good to involve people in experiences with handicapped persons, to develop not just compassion but understanding, and to change attitudes to this sector of our community. For in a sense we are all handicapped. It is merely a question of degree. And in a sense we all have somebody severely handicapped in our families or kinship groups — or will have, on the sheer law of probability.

"Our work in the school is important. Not only for the children here, who are, of course, central, but for the community as a whole. It is for this reason that I have been glad to play a large role in founding the Guild of Teachers of Backward Children, and that I have helped to promote both an Institute for Research and a College of Special Education.

"There is a terrific battle of ideas to be fought out in the teaching profession, as well as beyond it. I have taught classes of very bright children, and thoroughly enjoyed doing so; and I am aware of what is possible when the homes support the children, when the children are not handicapped, when classes are small — as they are in wealthy fee-paying schools. Yet I would like to see all school education child-centred and all university education student-centred and what a leading trade unionist called (in a different context) 'the arrogance of the intellectuals' transformed by the discovery that not all scholars are teachers, even though we would like all teachers to be scholars.

"I have had at times to disturb the Establishment. I don't mind doing that. Yet it is only fair to say that often my most enthusiastic support comes from the field-marshals of the Establishment. One comes to expect opposition more from the lance-corporals."

He did not say it, but in all education the chief enemy is neither field-marshal nor lance-corporal. It is apathy.

3 School as community

Fordham University Preparatory School
(Catholic). USA

In industrialized society, it is not only in the adult world that a sense of community is lacking. Even though a school is the last surviving institution where people meet and deal with people in a human way; even though, in consequence, a school is not as faceless as a corporation; it can and does have some of the same problems in trying to arrange that its members share a sense of community of interest, community of purpose, community of living.

And the situation is rendered the more difficult by the fact that many administrators of schools and of education systems have taken the industrial corporation as a model. At high levels, the talk is of the "knowledge industry" (a branch of the people industry). In the schools, it is easy for students to see themselves as attending from nine till four in order to fulfil an obligation imposed on them by society and then departing, rather like factory workers, to the dispersed foci of their real interests.

For the teachers, especially those in secondary schools, it is equally easy, in an age of tremendous pressure on educational personnel and facilities, to see their task as one of pouring out units of subject matter to consumer units — a clientele whom they know perhaps as well as the service station attendant knows his customers, but possibly no better.

In the name of economy and efficiency, the system may be geared to allow a minimum of "wastage" of employee time on interpersonal relationships; and the powerful ethos of the competitively acquisitive society does a great deal to persuade many teachers towards the "ideal" of giving as little as possible in exchange for the maximum financial return, since this is the ideal of the successful businessman and business institution in aiming to maximize profits.

Attempts to create a sense of community in schools take a

number of forms, from the harmless inanity of an annual speech night to the debatable institution of boarding schools. They include the wearing of a uniform, emphasis on school tradition, school sporting and cultural events, group methods of study, continuity of staffing, and pastoral care by house and form masters or their equivalents.

An alternative approach to all of this is to base a school on pre-existing community of interest. To a certain extent, such a procedure is inevitable in any school: all the members are human beings, which is a start; and most government systems use the neighbourhood as a basis for enrolment, a somewhat anachronistic organizational survival of an age when a neighbourhood was a community.

Again, the religious school, whatever its critics may think of it *qua* religious, can at least begin from a situation where its members hold much more in common, constitute a more cohesive social unit, than a randomly assorted group in a secular school. Whether it can always use this initial advantage constructively may be another question; but at least the opportunity is there, as anyone who has taught or studied in such a school can testify.

A complication is that in many countries the religious school has to be fully or largely self-supporting, so that it tends to be either significantly poorer than its State counterparts (when parents can afford only small fees) or considerably richer, when it is "taken up" by the well-to-do and becomes a snob school with or without much real religious spirit. Thus part of the sense of one-ness may be economic as well as religious. And part, too, in a few cases, may be the cohesiveness of a distinguishable minority.

Fordham Preparatory School is a Catholic academic day school for boys aged from 12 or 13 to about 18. It is tending towards a kind of bilateral co-education, with a nearby girls' school. Mt. St. Ursulane. Classes are mainly segregated, but some staff and facilities are shared.

All Fordham's courses are college preparatory ones. The school is located on the campus of Fordham University and its fees are $830 per year, so that its full-fee clientele must be at least middle-class and many are well-to-do.

I am going to assume here that the reader knows the sort of ideals of full character development, academic study and religious outlook that such a school would espouse. I shall content myself with adding that, as a Jesuit school, Fordham places the ideal of service close to the heart of its educational philosophy. All this being accepted, what else about the school is uniquely or unusually valuable or thought-provoking?

To begin with, Fordham is one of the few U.S. schools that are closely articulated with a university. The principal, the

Reverend Eugene J. O'Brien S.J., thought there might be a score such but certainly not fifty. The liaison is more than mere geography, and more than the fact that Fordham University is also a Catholic institution to which about 40% of the school's students proceed.

The school has a budget allocation from the university of just on $100,000 a year, which is used mainly to relieve some of the economic pressure on the less well-to-do students. This financial relationship is important of course; but more important is dialogue between the school and university faculties, with live discussion on integration of studies rather than a university consistently bemoaning the inefficiency of the high school, and a school lamenting university demands. Again, there are university staff members teaching high school students in final-year elective courses. About a quarter of the senior high school class are taking courses alongside Fordham University students and doing well, sometimes outstandingly well, compared with boys considerably senior to them.

Integration downwards, with the primary school that is, is even further developed.

"I don't think," said Father O'Brien, "that a private school of this kind has any right to exist at all, unless it is giving a lead in some way."

A lead that Fordham Prep. offers is its 7:3:3 plan. One of the U.S.A.'s common patterns of educational organization is the 8:4:4, the student spending 8 years in elementary and middle school, 4 years in high school, 4 years in college or university. For the academic student this pattern is virtually 8:4:4:2, or even 8:4:4:4, since two years and perhaps four of graduate study will usually follow the first degree. In the wealthy U.S. economy, this means that the student — even allowing for some vacation earning — is largely dependent for at least the first third of his life.

It is reasonable to wonder how much farther this process will go, and what will be the long-term characterological effects of such sustained dependency.

Fordham's present 7:3:3 modification of the pattern, linking elementary school, high school and college is not, basically, motivated by economics. "The point," I was told, "is not in the years saved, but in what is done with those years." The exercise will justify itself if there is real gain to the student who completes the standard sixteen years of schooling in thirteen years.

Lack of integration of different levels of education brings its train of difficulties into many forms of school organization that stress individual rates of progress. A child may complete a year's work in eight months and move on to the next grade. He may repeat the process; but if he eventually gets to be a year ahead of his age mates in the sequential academic subjects, there is generally nowhere for him to go. The school then proceeds to offer "enrichment" programs, which means extra subjects or broader treatment of topic areas already covered. Yet, if all the grades from kindergarten to college were under one roof, there would seem to be no strong case, academically, for having the student pause at the end of his sixth or eighth or tenth or twelfth year — any more than the fifth or seventh, ninth or eleventh — in order to get into step for transition to a new establishment. The arrangement has always been mainly organizational rather than educational.

In any case, the child who changes from elementary to high school may, for a variety of reasons, lose most of his age mates on the way. If he has the necessary academic, social and emotional maturity to make the change at twelve, it is not a substantially different operation from doing so at thirteen, especially if, as happens in Fordham's case, a number of his peers do so with him. The main problem is to know each student sufficiently well to make the best decision for him.

As things stand, some 150 of the preparatory school's 800 boys are presently on the 7:3:3 track, having come into it with the blessing of the elementary schools. They study in summer schools, making up extra units during the long (almost three months) vacations. One such summer school session must be spent in Europe by all Fordham students as part of whatever linguistic-cultural studies are included in the boy's course. If he goes on to Fordham University, another European summer school will be a compulsory part of his course. At the end of three years, the 7:3:3 student is ready to proceed to any U.S.A. college, at age sixteen. His 8:4:4 colleague, of course, will be eighteen.

I sat in on a discussion-type English lesson with some thirteen-year-olds. A project was being developed around the possibility of patenting and selling a particular type of fighting kite. Although the venture was to be a genuine one, the project seemed to have some difficulty in getting off the ground. The ethic was extremely American, and I wondered, not for the first time or in the first country, just how far it is possible to go and still be "teaching English".

With a senior group I listened and joined in during a social studies session. The teacher had made the objective point that government tax money, collected mainly from the upper socio-economic classes, was also spent in their interests. He instanced the many still-segregated schools and the very high costs of building and maintaining good motorways to which the poorer classes would presumably give a pretty low priority. He and I were persuaded that the taxation system could be more effectively used as a means of redistribution of wealth; but the boys at this level, or at least the chief protagonists in the discussion, again maintained a traditional U.S. ethic: it was the middle class's money, so why shouldn't it be spent as the middle class wanted? Argument waxed warm.

At the end of the lesson I talked with a small group of these boys. Suppose I had sat in on a lesson in religion: Would it be possible for a stranger like myself to come in late to such a lesson and, not knowing what subject was set down on the time-table, assume that he was in a non-religious discussion on ethics? "Yes," thought some. Another suggested that the newcomer would know the subject was religion, even if no specifically religious issues came up, since the values being expressed were Christian ones. I demurred, offering to argue that my own secular position on the taxation issue was more Christian than that of my (and the teacher's) opponents. Anyhow, I asked, wouldn't the school be a better place educationally if it employed a few howling atheists? Wasn't it a closed society intellectually? There was some agreement. Another lad suggested that, even though he might agree also, there was a very liberal range of thought and opinion among the staff; and he reminded me that religion was an optional course for senior students. "But," responded one of the group, "you have it driven right into you in the elementary school, long before you get to Fordham."

Part of the school's trouble, I was told by a senior staff member, is that many of the boys are more theologically sophisti-cated than their parents, who hold B.A. and M.A. degrees but are products of a more traditional schooling and are themselves in need of religious re-education. Which, of course, was not always a message easy to convey with magnificent charm and tact to those parents who stood most in need.

When the school decided to give a series of lessons on drug education, the course was taken with parents first. Later it was included in science, though psychological, emotional and spiritual aspects came up for discussion.

Sex education is regarded by Fordham as a necessary part of schooling. But, asked Father O'Brien, is twelve already too late? Not prophylactically, but have deep and abiding attitudes already been formed? (Is four too late? Most sex education seems to be sex de-mis-education.)

I discussed this problem of sex education at some length with the lay teacher of theology (70% of Fordham's teaching staff are laymen) into whose ambit it came.

"These boys," he explained, "are middle-class and con-formist. Their words and their behaviour are vastly different. They admire the hippies from afar but it would take a stupendous effort of moral courage for them to renounce their whole upbringing and join them."

So his first problem with freshmen is to relieve them of an often very deeply ingrained guilt complex over masturbation, reassuring them that in their situation the moral implications, if any, are unimportant.

In the teenage stage — the 14-plus to 16-years-old sophomores and juniors — interest in heterosexual behaviour is strong. Anonymous questionnaires produce, invariably, the standard questions, "How far can I go with a girl?" "Is petting all right?" "Is premarital intercourse wrong?"

Now these, he tells the boys, are the wrong questions. They are not valid. They are questions that seek an authoritarian answer to obey, or to defy, or both. And ethical behaviour is not a matter of responding to authority. "We are in an inductive and not a deductive moral era." The problems of sexual behaviour are to be solved by building a total value system, and then placing one's sexuality within it.

A number of articles by acknowledged writers in the field are read, studied and discussed. They are frank enough, but converge quite definitely on a line of thought: that extra-marital sex is wrong, if not for all of the old reasons, then for some of them: that a boy can play at love and sex but a girl cannot, even though she imagines she can; that a casual relationship that may leave the boy emotionally unscathed may leave her permanently, psychologically scarred; and that the boy, once aware of this, can no longer seek his own gratification at the risk of such cost to his partner.

Privately the teacher admits that he thinks it possible that adults may be able to handle extra-marital sexual relationships, but that adolescents almost certainly cannot; for which reason he himself baulks at sexual freedom for adolescents, and feels that society and the family have an obligation to provide a framework of moral security in a time when the mass media are becoming increasingly "open-minded".

It is honest, no-holds discussion, taken co-educationally and successfully with Mt. St. Ursulane girls, and the strongest attack on the liberal-conventional view comes from the intelligent student who claims "You grew up in conditions that were so different from ours that your experience is no longer relevant".

It was the senior boys themselves who volunteered the information that they saw the school as a community. "We want to learn," said one, "and the teachers are helping us." And my thoughts flashed to the very different structure of the experimental gymnasium in Oslo. A boy whose mother had died the week before told me that 30 teachers out of the 90 on the Fordham faculty had attended the funeral, along with over 100 of the 800 students: this in a geographically scattered school community. For myself, I am no funeral-goer; but amongst the fraternity of funeral-goers, how many in an ordinary neighbourhood school would feel moved to attend on such an occasion?

I asked Father O'Brien for an overview of Fordham's work. He stressed freedom of method, experimentation, relationships between staff and students and the abandonment of the hard-line, monolithic approach to religious doctrine and life problems.

"The school aims," he said, "to produce somebody who can think independently and with some degree of creativity; who can make judgements about the significant things in life with confidence, and after careful scrutiny; and who sees his life as one of service to his fellowmen. Balance he should have, and a sense of humour. But the hallmark of the school is joyful commitment to service.

"As for the teaching faculty, Jesuit and layman alike, our function is to bring a dimension of conviction and commitment to our fellowman, in this case children and their parents, by what we are and do, as one of the experiences in their lives — as an example; but then we must leave them free to choose."

I asked whether he would feel that the school had failed if the students had acquired all of those things but rejected the religious dimension.

"Yes," said Father O'Brien. "I would. But I would feel also that it had failed if religious belief had to be **imposed**." And he added, "The presence of religion is to bear witness to Christ's example of service".

I suspect that in a world being polarized by moral crisis the greatest ecumenical movement is likely to be a rapprochement between religious and secular defenders of the same liberal humane values. Nothing that I saw or heard in Fordham ran contrary to such a belief. Very much seemed to confirm it.

4 Midword:*
a study in almost still life

Harold X. is a student at the government school in Sometown.

For the major part of every school day, Harold sits at a steel-framed, heavy-timbered double desk which cramps his adolescent legs between book-rack and floor, contorts and squeezes his adolescent body and compels him into postural error and long-term risk of minor physical deformity whenever he has to write or calculate.

The too-smallness and inconvenience of Harold's desk are symbolic of many things. If desk tops were large enough to hold a work book and a geography text and an atlas and writing materials all at one time, then not only would they cost more, but classrooms would need to be larger, so that governments would have to spend much more money to build them and parents would have to pay more taxes and buy fewer expensively advertised luxuries, from alcohol and cigarettes to latest model refrigerators, television sets and motor-cars. And since nothing is too good for our children, Harold gets — nothing. Nothing, that is, beyond the bare minimal necessities of schooling.

And if the book-rack were taken out from under Harold's desk, to allow seat and writing surface to be put in physically healthful relationship to each other, then more space again would be needed, in order that he might store his books and materials on shelves or in cupboards or lockers. And space costs money, tax money, the money of breadwinners who, as trades unionists and voters, zealously guard their own working conditions.

Of course a lot can be done by using variable-height single

* This should normally have been a foreword; but nobody reads forewords.
—H.P.S.

tables or desks and variable-height chairs; but even these raise the awful space-expense problem. Nevertheless, Harold's government is beginning to introduce better furniture into some of its newest schools. The trouble is that Harold is in one of his country's several hundreds of older schools, schools which contain scores of thousands of older desks that have twenty or thirty years of solid, serviceable life built into them and to ask any conscientious public servant to replace these items at a cost of three or four or five million dollars of the taxpayers' money merely so that Harold may sit in comfort and physical safety would be patently absurd. You might just as unreasonably ask the defence department to sell at bargain rates twenty or thirty million dollars' worth of fully serviceable, expensive bombing planes, merely because designers had come up with more efficient ways of gassing and incinerating and infecting and disintegrating the currently designated enemies of Harold's country. Or do defence departments do just this?

So Harold sits, if sitting is exactly the word for the position he adopts, reasonably motionless at his desk. And the desk remains motionless in the room, because the janitor doesn't like finding desks out of place, and because books and materials clatter off their racks onto the floor when desks are being moved, but chiefly because Harold's teachers don't really see any point in shifting furniture (and it can be so shifted even in a cramped room) so as to seat students in small study groups and in large discussion circles and big drama-watching horse-shoes.

Harold's teachers are, after all, the key to all else. Many of them are earnest people (though some of them are not) and none of them, this year, could possibly be called inspiring. Well-intentioned usually, kind to "children" (often as distinct from "students") they have been ground to a shape that society demands and is prepared to pay for. Undertrained, underqualified, lacking in the deep professional insight that is the product of long preparatory study, they are therefore routinized, unimaginative, and dull — oh, so terribly dull!

Day after day they turn, and Harold turns at their behest, to the next dust-dry page of dead information and deadly drill, prescribed by some higher authority and laid out in neat little lesson-slabs like the daily regimen of the city gaol. The diet is revolting; but the teachers do not revolt, for they have been conditioned over the decades to accept their places as alienated servants of the impersonal instruction machine that serves the ends of the State and of industry and commerce; and Harold does not revolt either, because the whole vast, impersonal weight of the organized State is against him, telling him that this is legally compulsory education; and the emotional weight of his home is heavy on Harold, as parents urge that he must work hard and

memorize more and write out his drills and exercises so that
he may pass his examinations, which are the sole purpose of
"education", in order that he may qualify for a well-paid niche
in the super-State and be able to buy his children blue bonnet-
ribbons, and house-room, and beautiful plastic gewgaws, and
tooth-destroying confectionery — and a dull, dull, dull education.

Now not all schools are like this. Not all of any country's
classrooms are stolidly constrictive age cages, stuffy in summer,
draughty in winter, and drab all the year round, with forty children
herded into space for twenty-five while bored and boring teachers
pour forth predigested "education" like programmed robots interminably grinding out relentless streams of bone dust. Though I
believe that Harold and his classroom are unexaggerated proto-
types, I am sure that there are, in every country, other classrooms
where, for other Harolds, learning is gay, active, humane, exciting,
insightful, a reciprocal relationship between enthusiastic teachers
and willing learners. I am equally sure that, in most countries,
such classrooms are inestimably fewer than children have a right
to expect and parents a duty to demand.

I know something about the overall picture here, since I
spend a not inconsiderable fraction of my life in moving round
schools and observing what goes on in them. As a result of a
world trip, made possible by generous study leave provisions by
Monash University, I now know more than I did about some
"schools" — the term is used rather loosely to cover a wide range
of educational institutions, where important, exciting and different
things are being done. And it was in order to share with others
— parents and teachers — involved in the education of children
and adolescents that this book was written.

Between "having written a book" and "being in the throes
of writing a book" the difference, from the viewpoint of the spec-
tator, is roughly the same as that between possessing children and
being pregnant: nothing could have exceeded the courtesy and
kindness with which overworked people in important positions
made time for a fly-by-night academic who wanted to visit and
discuss their schools for a day or so. Since there were often
half-a-dozen teachers, principals and administrators involved in
arranging and assisting each visit, I do not propose to try to list
them all here.

Nor shall I attempt to name all those who helped by reading
the manuscript chapters I forwarded for their criticism and comment. Their contribution was invaluable. Sometimes it was merely
a matter of correcting a vital statistic or two. In another case, one
principal has more or less re-written my chapter completely.
Astonishing though it may sound, there was scarcely an objection
raised to the often quite critical remarks I had made: if my facts
were wrong, they were corrected; if my opinions were tart, that

was my business; so, in effect, they said unanimously. To them, and to my other helpers in four continents, my warmest thanks are due. To those whose schools were crowded out of this book by considerations of space and cost and other factors, I am equally grateful and also apologetic.

Finally, I must thank expressly my paper, *The Australian*, for permission to use material previously published in abbreviated form in its columns.

I believe all the schools I have described to be good schools. I am not suggesting that they are the seventeen best schools in the world, or that somebody else could not make a similar trip to mine and find a quite different selection. Nor is there any implication that the schools are necessarily the best in their countries, or somehow representative of them (except in ways that have occasionally been indicated in the text). The concept is as simple as the title: these are "Good Schools", schools that I believe all the teachers and parents of all the Harolds ought to know about in order that they may have some models of better education for Harold and some evidence that good things are already being done.

Finally, I should add that I have described the schools as I saw them at a particular time, during the calendar year 1968. In a changing world, some of them will have changed significantly in at least some respects before my descriptions of them are read. Nevertheless, I have striven for as much truthfulness as a necessarily brief visit and the revisions of my colleagues in each school allow, and for obvious stylistic reasons have elected to use the present tense rather than a clumsy past one. Essentially, each account is honest and correct, so far as it goes. Man that is a creature within space and time can do no more.

H. P. Schoenheimer.

December, 1969.

5 Mail way

A roasting hot November afternoon in Charleville, South-west Queensland. I was seated at my classroom table filling in railway concession forms for Ray, an intelligent fourteen-year-old student, resident in the local Church of England hostel.

"Where do you live, Ray?" I enquired, busily writing.

"Winton, sir," said Ray, naming a town far to our north.

Surprised, I stopped and looked up. Winton had its own school.

"What, right in Winton?"

"Oh, no, sir — couple of hundred miles out."

Of Australia's twelve million inhabitants spread over three million square miles, rather more than seven million are in the six State capitals and most of the rest live in the narrow eastern coastal strip. Sydney, with two-and-a-half million inhabitants is a throbbing modern metropolis, larger than Rome or Washington. Melbourne, with two millions and a quarter, shades Toronto, Karachi and Athens.

In compensation, Australia's semi-arid and desert inland areas are inevitably sparsely populated. Thargomindah has always been a conspicuous dot on the map of Queensland. When I taught there, six hundred miles from the coast, 150 miles from the nearest railhead, it had a population of 70, with a one-room school holding twenty pupils. Men and women from the vast sheep and cattle stations farther out called us folk of Thargomindah, "You lucky b's on the inside".

Australia is dotted with hundreds of Thargomindahs and specked with thousands of lonely grazing properties. So, necessarily, it has become expert at educating from a distance. Each State Education Department has a Correspondence School serving

36

children of the distant outback where a family may live fifty miles from the nearest neighbour.

Because control of education in Australia is very highly centralized, each correspondence section operates from the State capital.

In 1968 the Queensland Primary Correspondence School, which is located in Brisbane, enrolled rather more than two and a half thousand students, of whom approximately 200 were adults completing a long-delayed primary education. The rest tended to cluster towards the five-to-nine-years end of the school. Older country children can travel further to school, even as far as thirty miles each way by bus in a long school day.

Since Brisbane is located in the extreme south-eastern corner of a State that occupies two-thirds of a million square miles, the distances involved in correspondence education are immense.

Cheryl and Peter are ten-year-old twins living nearly a thousand miles away to the west of Brisbane. Their lesson sheets go into the mail bag in Brisbane and travel 650 miles by rail to the terminus at Quilpie. Here they are picked up by a local aircraft and flown another three hundred miles to lonely Arnewarra Station. In due course, completed lessons will go back over the same route for the teacher's assessment and comments. And these in turn will find their way back to Arnewarra, two hundred miles from the nearest school building.

> *Dear Mr. James,*
>
> *I am afraid the children's last sets of lessons are somewhere at the bottom of the Paroo River. My husband was driving us through the floods in the jeep on our return from the township when the force of the floodwaters tipped the vehicle over on its side. The mail was in one of the coolie baskets and the baby was in the other, and both went floating away on the water. We decided to save the baby, and the mail had to go. Can you please send us extra work, including duplicates of the last lot, in the next mail?*
>
> *Yours sincerely,*
> *Mrs. E. Darrell.*

A thousand miles is a long way for lessons to travel. But Thursday Island, at the northern tip of Queensland and Australia, is a good 400 miles further than that; and from Brisbane to inland New Guinea, where many Queenslanders are temporarily or semi-permanently resident far from regular schooling, lessons fly for distances of a thousand miles and a half. The big brown envelopes wing off, too, to Julie of Grade 6 in Tucson, Arizona, where her father, a TV cameraman, has a long-term assignment; to David, in Grade 2, care of the Banco Interamericano de Desarollo Group, Asesor de Comibol, Bolivia, where father has a diplomatic posting; to Christopher in Grade 3, in the Diocese of Melanesia,

Tawaniara, British Solomon Islands; and to Keith, Grade 1, in Talawakelle, Ceylon, and to Eileen and Graham in Assam, and to Alison and Christine in Lufi Lufi, Western Samoa — mainly missionary families, these.

Composition

"My parents came to New Guinea in 1956 and I was born in 1958. Eight native boys took turns carrying Mother to the nearest air-strip which is thirty-three miles away, because the hospital is at the coast and we live in the Highlands. Mother was carried in a canvas chair tied to bamboo poles. I came home from the hospital in a small screened-in box with four boys carrying me."

Teaching through the mail has its own techniques, based on the usual principles, but requiring additional specialized know-how.

Lessons are carefully prepared, detailed step by detailed step, with much emphasis on visual material. Where the child is too young to read the instructions himself, a typical lesson will consist of four or five offset-printed foolscap sheets containing both the reading, writing, number, art and so on for the child, and the instructions for the Home Supervisor. She is usually the mother but sometimes, on a more wealthy homestead, a governess.

"Dear Miss Crane:

I am sorry that Donald and Janet have not completed all their assignments for this week. They are the eldest of four children, all working at different levels. I have a new baby, and as it is the height of the shearing season I am particularly busy just now, cooking for my husband and the men. I have had to leave the elder children to fend for themselves and give what time I can to supervising Ronnie and Elwyn who seem to need a lot of help. I will try to see that Donald and Janet catch up on their work by next week.

With best wishes and thanks,
Yours faithfully,
(Mrs.) B. Sandhurst."

Governesses — fifty-four of them — from the four corners and the wide centre of Queensland — came to a three-weeks' seminar in Brisbane, where they were given a crash course in teaching methods and child management by teachers of the correspondence school and training college lecturers. Instant pedagogy, perhaps, but at least a beginning. For other home supervisors, who may be governesses or mothers, there are one-day seminars in larger country towns.

Forty weeks' detailed lessons in each of a wide range of subjects — reading, writing, spelling, literature, mathematics, social studies, sewing, art, craft — all at seven different grade levels: these, prepared by experienced teachers, become the pedagogic capital of the Primary Correspondence School. Unlike its counterpart in neighbouring New South Wales, Queensland P.C.S. has never been able to afford such luxuries as printed lessons with colour illustrations, or suitable materials for the teaching of a full science curriculum.

Nature, however, surrounds these children of the outback, and their letters and compositions are crammed with tales of owl and dingo and wild pigs and the fish in the big lagoon. One teacher received in the weekly mail a well-crated, well-fed barking lizard. Another got a huge butterfly collection. A third took to the museum for identification a well-preserved bush mouse of unusual species. A fourth decided that the museum was the best repository for some very uninhibited native carvings from the Sepik River area of New Guinea.

Yet we live in times of rapid change, and the new mathematics and new methods in English and a changing social studies world are reflected in new or revised lessons. To the outsider, the load on the P.C.S. staff seems heavy. Seventy Grade One children are allotted to one teacher, 65 Grade Two's, and so on up to 25 Grade Seven's. This means half-an-hour to read, check, and assess one infant's work, to think about the strengths and weaknesses displayed, and to indicate to the home supervisor what remedial action seems to be the best in the circumstances. For a twelve-to-thirteen-year-old who pours out a reasonable volume of work, the teacher can spare eighty minutes or so per week. And even these figures are based on the assumption that the teacher does no preparation of lessons, no professional reading, no letter-writing to pupils and supervisors and participates in no conferences with colleagues. As I found on visiting the P.C.S., the teachers do all of these things. P.C.S. staff also have absences due to illness, since often it is the teacher whose health is not adequate who finds his way into correspondence teaching. In all the circumstances, a change to an overall pupil-staff ratio such as obtains in the day schools would not appear over-generous.

As settlement spreads and motor transport annihilates distance, enrolments in the primary correspondence school may be expected to decline still further. (Today's two-and-a-half thousand is only half of the figure of a decade earlier.) But there is no foreseeable time when the really distant places will not need the school. And there will always be children who, either temporarily or permanently, are too ill or incapacitated to attend day school, and for these the P.C.S. caters also. Sometimes, indeed, children labour under disadvantages of both sickness and distance.

"*Dear Mr. Nixon:*

I write, I hope not too self-pityingly, to explain the present situation with Andrew and Lachlan.

As you may remember, both of them are haemophiliacs.

This means that with their type of disease, there are long periods up to several weeks when they must be confined to their beds and cannot study. When they are well, like most little boys of their age (eight and ten), they want to play, especially if the weather is warm and bracing, as it is now. I try hard to impress on them the necessity for long hours of study when they have the strength and energy, but they are such children, and it is a great strain for them and for me.

Miss Westmoreland, a retired teacher who acts as governess on Silver Downs station, now comes over to the house twice a week. This was Andrew's and Lachlan's first contact with a real, live teacher. . . .

I also have another son, Gerald, aged six. We have had the 'fun' of the new Cuisenaire mathematics this year, and sometimes I have felt that I was going quite dotty. However, the penny has dropped for both mother and child, and now we are all enjoying it!

I haven't any help when the elder boys are ill . . ."

On every school day except Friday, the network of national radio stations that covers Queensland broadcasts primary correspondence lessons. These are keyed to material already supplied to the pupils; and the teachers — some but not all of the P.C.S. staff — use a friendly conversational approach. For a talk about Tasmania, for example, the child already has had supplied a stencilled map of that State, with physical features marked in and numbers 1 to 12 for reference to specific places. The sheet gives the date of the broadcast (Thursday, 25th July, 1968), title of lesson and teacher (Grade 4 — Miss Dartington — Social Studies) and instructions to have atlas, pencil and sheet ready. There are similar sheets for a wide range of lessons: illustrated nursery rhymes for Grade I and mathematics for Grade 5, and general science for Grades 5 to 7, and even handwork (matchbox modelling and colour marbling) for Grade 2. And so on, over the syllabus.

"To answer my next two questions, boys and girls, you'll probably need to glance quickly at both of the Cuisenaire staircases you have built.
Does 7 minus 3 equal 6 minus 2? . . . Yes, it does.
Why is 7 minus 3 equal to 6 minus 2? . . . Did you say, 'Because they both equal 4?'
Is 18 minus 14 equal to 15 minus 11? . . . How do you know they're equal? . . . They're both equal to 4. Very good.
Now, return all the rods to the pile and push them aside so that you've a large, clear space to do Mr. Forsayth's work on sets and Venn diagrams."

". . . Good morning, Grade 2 . . ."

By medium and short wave, the school broadcasts have reached most of the correspondence students. But it is one-way communication, and desperately difficult to keep from sounding artificial.

"Stand back, stand back I say!"
"Oh, Derek, you'll be killed!"
"See, the dragon is breathing fire!"
"Whoooosh!"

. . . .
"Susan!"
"I'm sorry, Miss Whitlock, I couldn't hear the dragon at all."
"Neither could I, at least not properly. Simon, have you been letting your batteries go flat again?"

The little drama is remarkable mainly in that no member of the cast is within ten miles of another. The conditions for joining one of the three most exclusive schools in the world are simple enough: you must be enrolled with the Primary Correspondence School; you have to live at least 100 miles from Charleville or Charters Towers or Mount Isa; and you have to own, or hire from the Queensland Education Department, a two-way radio apparatus known locally as a transceiver.

There are just on three hundred pupils of the Schools of the Air, roughly a hundred in each. On precious air time, when the wavelengths are "lent" to them by the Royal Flying Doctor Service, teachers in the three centres conduct class lessons with their unseen pupils. Time allotments vary, but usually each class gets a daily lesson, varying in length from half an hour to an hour. Some lessons follow the syllabuses in the basic subjects, English, mathematics, social studies. Some are pupil talks on geography and nature. Some are drama and recitation. There are agricultural project clubs that "meet" on the transceivers so that members can report on the state of their vegetable crops, read the financial statement of moneys disbursed for seed and fertilizer and moneys received from mothers for carrots or radishes, and pass on useful information gleaned from experience and reading.

Mt. Isa's School of the Air pupils are terribly far-scattered, even by Queensland's generous standard, and Mt. Isa's two S.O.T.A. teachers envy those of Charters Towers and Charleville who are able (with how much painstaking care and effort from all involved the reader is now in a position to understand) to arrange annual gatherings of their pupils. Charters Towers had its School Camp on nearby (100 miles) Magnetic Island, followed by a buffet dinner and concert in Charters Towers itself and the school's own Sports Day. Charleville runs its sports day on a "house" basis, in the town.

"When the schools in Charters Towers had their annual

sports day, School of the Air competed.

Arriving at the show grounds where the sports were to be held at 9 a.m., we found a number of children there and others arriving all the time. For a while all was hustle and bustle as parents and children met each other.

Then we were given our sashes with the letters 'S.O.T.A.' printed in white on maroon. These looked very striking.

Miss Saxton, our School of the Air teacher, with the help of some parents soon had us out on the field practising ball games and races. In the first race and throughout the day we gained four third places. This may not seem much in points but we all thoroughly enjoyed the experience of taking part in competitive sports. Although we came last in all the ball games, Miss Saxton said we did so well with only a little practice, we'd have beaten the schools with a week's practice."

So the tenuous threads stretch from the wide, isolated properties to link the children of the primary correspondence school to the larger world and to one another. There is a lending library of 9000 volumes, a school badge with the motto "Success Crowns Effort". There were for many years Junior Red Cross circles.

For the School Dental Service, a Dental Clinic incessantly follows the great spiderweb of Queensland's railway network and a solitary car-borne dentist rides the remoter roadways, meeting appointments made months in advance from a distance of hundreds of leagues. On request, you can have Sunday School lessons by correspondence.

Each year some students make trips to the Brisbane Exhibition (Queensland's State Fair); and P.C.S. handwriting and embroidery and mapping and art are liberally represented among the winners of blue and red and green ribbons at the local fairs of country towns. At Christmas the P.C.S. sends a Christmas card and gift book to every pupil, and little tributes of ties and handkerchiefs and perfume (and local fauna) come back, in the wake of end-of-the-year examination papers, by train, boat, truck, packhorse, van, camel, aeroplane and canoe.

Yearly, too, there is a printed magazine, "Mail Way" from which I have filched the title for this chapter. It contains numerous photographs of P.C.S. children, many examples of art, and scores of samples of prose and verse writing.

"A snake bit me on the toe and I screamed. Mummy cut the bite and tied a piece of rope around my leg. Daddy drove me to hospital and it took us three hours. I liked being in hospital. The nurses were nice."

"The old sailor on the sea wall
Was weaving, with his hands

And with his mind,
Nets of memory,
And nets of twine.
He liked to think of his memories as nets
For the breeze to blow through
In salt-stream abandon —
Yet in their mesh he knew
Were certain sea-pearls,
Caught fast by anchors of remembrance;
The treasures of his life's experience."

"*Our home stands on a grassy hill surrounded by beautiful mountains and bushlands. Nearby there is a lagoon, three miles long, which, in spring time is covered with pretty waterlilies. Our property consists of five hundred square miles of grassy paddocks, in which Hereford cattle graze. There are some bottle trees near our homestead. We have recently had some scrub pulled and the paddocks are looking lovely now. Some other paddocks have been ringbarked and there is now more water for the cattle. The Moolayember Creek began to flow, after nearby trees were ringbarked.*

Our favourite swimming hole, which is almost thirty feet deep in some places, is in the nearby lagoon. We swim in the cool shaded water during the weekends and after school.

In our small sheep paddock, we keep a few Border Leicester sheep for domestic use.

On Warrinilla, we have an airstrip. Often, aeroplanes land on it. Six miles away on our property, an oil rig has been erected.

Our school house is a short distance from the main homestead. It used to be a married couple's quarters. In our school room, we have pinned maps and charts onto the walls. These help us with our work. We are very lucky to have such a delightful place in which to do our school work."

The Blue Gums

"*The creek is gurgling mid rock and sand,*
Along its banks the blue gums stand.
I see them standing there so tall,
And from their boughs the magpies call.
White their trunks and leaves of green,
About their roots the ibis preen.
Towards the end of day,
This is where the dingoes play."

What happens after primary school? Some of the children go to a boarding school for secondary education. There is a secondary correspondence school, considerably larger than the P.C.S.

It is possible, at least in theory, to complete all of one's schooling, from infant class to final university year, by correspondence, and Queensland University does indeed have many thousands of graduates who (like myself) graduated five hundred or a thousand miles from the campus.

In the undeveloped world, education at a distance has a different role to play. In correspondence education in Queensland and the other Australian States, the mother, as home supervisor, is a key person. In Asia and Africa she will herself have no formal education. It may be that use will be made of a quite different "mix" of printed visual material with radio, since television will be a long time spreading. It may be necessary to "seed" villages and farms with literate people, possibly peripatetics as many early Australian schoolteachers were.

There is still a lot of scope in the world for learning the mail way. There are still many people who swear by it.

"Dear Mr. Biggs:

My garden is comeing on fine, the pigs are all pretty good exept one, she bit me on the third finger from the right on the right hand. We now have 60 pigs and soon hope to have 78 of them. Dad hopes to move up to A. at the end of August, it will be a sad day when I have to leave the Primery Correspondence School and go to a sticken State School in that dump of a town of A. . . ."

6 No compulsory leaving age

Folkhighschools. Sweden

(i) SIGTUNA

Sweden refers to those of its adults who left school at fifteen as "the lost generation". It does so even though the best estimates are that, each year, at least one adult in ten is involved in some form of regular, organized popular (i.e. non-vocational) education. Wage-earners and their families predominate. Many manual workers participate.

For as far ahead as one can read the future of any nation, adult education is destined to become increasingly important. In a technologically changing world, re-training for one's old or new vocation will inevitably occupy considerably more time. In a politically and socially changing world, continuing deep study, by adults, of political and social affairs must become an essential aspect of living if democracy is to survive. In an automated world, increasing leisure will create, in any population that has not been de-educated in the schools, an increasing demand for opportunity to study the cultural heritage enshrined in literature and the arts and to learn to create in such fields.

There is a reason of a somewhat different genre why adult education is likely to remain important for a very long time indeed. Sooner or later, young people want to move into the world and live as fully responsible members of the community. For some adolescents this stage comes sooner rather than later, whether for reasons of temperament or uninspiring education or a combination of these and other factors is not always clear. What happens to them in the bright new world?

In most countries, the present pattern of educational organization is such as to discourage return to study in later years, making it economically difficult as well as highly demanding of time and energy. Usually the pattern is one of part-time work after a day's occupation. Yet there is much evidence to suggest that the person who does return is more strongly motivated, more efficient in learning, better able to relate theoretical study to the world he knows and the goals he sets himself in that world. One common and conspicuous example is the veteran given a new educational start after return from a war. Another is the typical student of a Swedish folk high school.

The folk high school movement began in Denmark in the 1840's. Its purpose was then, as to a large extent it still remains, the personal and social development of those adults who voluntarily joined it for study in the evenings and in winter months, even at considerable economic sacrifice. Sweden adopted and adapted the concept, adding more practical dimensions of a civic and vocational nature, and developing to the present residential pattern.

Today Sweden has just over a hundred folk high schools, almost half of which are organized and administered by County Councils. The remainder are run by voluntary organizations as widely different as the Blue Ribbon (Christian temperance) movement, the Young Farmers' Association and the Salaried Employees' Educational Association, an offshoot of the strongly left-wing trade union movement. Religious nonconformists, political Conservatives and YMCA's also sponsor folk high schools; so do the labour movement and the universities.

Of the 13,000 students in Swedish folk high schools, most are young people aged within a year or two of 22. In Sigtuna, one of the oldest and most famous institutions, I asked 89 of these young men and women, the question: "Now that you have had the experience of leaving school and returning to study again, what advice would you give to a person who was undecided: to do as you have done, or to study straight through?" As it turned out, only 67 of the 89 had indeed left and returned, and of these only 8 suggested studying straight through. The other 22 had simply come to a folk high school rather than to a normal secondary school, and of them two-thirds (14) had decided that they, too, should have left school and come back later.

A stern solid-brick castle, Sigtuna Folkhogskola stands on a rise above Sigtuna township, a half-hour's car-drive from Stockholm, looking exactly what it is, a bastion of the Swedish Church. Austerely set, it looks across fields of winter snow to Lake Malar beyond. The steps that lead up to the castle door are of yellow granite and the cloisters surround a quadrangle with a summer rose-garden. The dominant note of austerity reaches into hall and lecture-rooms, into chapel and cellars, up the spiral stone stairway to the rocky turret room and down by more twining steps to the library in the basement.

Sigtuna Stiftelsen (Sigtuna Foundation) is controlled by a

board that includes representatives of temperance bodies and the Student Christian Movement as well as other church organizations for lay workers. On the same site as the folk high school is state-supported Sigtuna Boarding School for 400 boys and girls, more English than the English, offering a very traditional classical-humanist education.

The folk high school has an enrolment of between 100 and 110 students. As in most such schools now, women outnumber men by about 60 to 40. Students come from different social levels (many FHS have students who are almost all industrial or almost all farming workers) but the great majority seemed to be seeking higher qualifications for vocational purposes. There is a sprinkling of students — about ten — from a quite wide geographical range: Denmark, Norway, Iceland, Finland, U.S.A., Spain, Lebanon, Greece. Interestingly, a small group of the Swedish students are from Stockholm, finding the boarding life of Sigtuna more relaxing than the pressures of daily school.

Sigtuna is chiefly remarkable, not for the nature of its educational activities, but for very liberal government support for what is, in effect, a new lease of educational life for the students.

All of the salaries and pensions of all folkhighschool teachers are paid by the State, at the ruling rates for teachers, and with staffing schedules rather more generous than the generous ones prevailing in the schools. The staff at Sigtuna includes seven full-time teachers in addition to the principal. The State meets, also, 75% of building costs. Students must pay 330 kronor (about $66 U.S.) per month for board and lodging and can receive back, according to their circumstances, up to two-thirds of this amount from the State as a non-repayable grant; they may also borrow up to 5000 kronor ($1000 U.S.) per academic year on long-term (20 years), at 3% interest, with repayments commencing after a three-year moratorium. No personal guarantee or collateral is required. Sigtuna students from other Scandinavian countries receive similar financial support from their homelands.

In Sigtuna, as in other folkhighschools, courses run for 34 weeks of the year, from September to June. Most students take a two-year course, a few return for a third year. All folkhighschools must include Swedish, history and social science in their curricula for two years and mathematics and science for a least one. Religion, however, is an optional study. Different folkhighschools may decide to add other compulsory studies. Additional course offerings in Sigtuna and elsewhere are such as to make it possible for the students to complete what are, in effect, the last two years of the nine-year comprehensive school.

There is no examination at the end of the course. When a student has completed it he gets a certificate to say so and may use this either as an employment qualification or to obtain entry to a continuation school or a vocational school, where he is entitled to the same liberal State support. On the other hand, a few students, but only a few, come from these two institutions for a year's study at Sigtuna.

Folkhighschools have deep roots in the Scandinavian communities. In earlier times, before the present deep, wide, and warm educational blanket spread so completely over the land, they provided an irreplaceable and invaluable route for able and disadvantaged people to repair the gaps in their education. Several members of the present parliament have a folkhighschool background. Dan Anderson, Vilhelm Moberg, and Harry Blomberg are renowned Swedish writers who came up the hard way — elementary school, folkhighschool, private study. Werner Aspenström, a poet and dramatist, and Stig Sjöden, a poet, studied in Sigtuna a generation ago and still pay occasional visits to the school's guesthouse. One highly placed official of the National Board of Education is a Sigtuna alumnus.

Teaching at Sigtuna is largely on traditional lines, the small classes making for a tutorial atmosphere. Classes begin at 8.15 a.m. and continue until 10.45 a.m. when the normal, early Scandinavian lunch is taken. After lunch, there is a study break until 1.45, followed by a full afternoon of classes, with dinner at 4.50 p.m.

This leaves a long, free evening which is given over to voluntary "study circles", a wide term meaning groups assembled for anything from folk dancing, drama and music to study of government affairs or extra mathematics.

Another strand is aesthetics, a three-year course, in which all students must participate for at least the first year. This is an experimental year, given over to creating from colour, material, and sound (which is regarded as material for composition). Groups spend some time listening to silence, identifying sounds in the environment, combining them, recording the result, hearing, criticizing and improving on their efforts. Voices are used, not with rhythm and melody, but to produce sounds that can be consciously patterned. From here there is a lead to "new" music and thence to more conventional music heard and discussed as immediate experience, not in relation to "book" training and criticism. Classical music, "pop", jazz, baroque, modern all have a part.

The library of 75,000 volumes is large for a school of 100 or so, but quite its most remarkable feature is its carefully filed and cross-indexed collection of two million newspaper cuttings dating from 1918. This is Sweden's oldest and largest collection, covering 16 newspapers, kept up-to-date by a band of devoted ladies, and widely used by academic staff and students of nearby Uppsala university. The original sombreness of the dungeon-like location is to some extent relieved by (in addition to the ladies) two contrasting features: a variety of brightly coloured modern paintings and a range of stolid notabilities in restrained photographic sepia.

The ultimate *raison d'etre* for Sigtuna remains its religious commitment. Nowadays, little use is made of the picturesque open-air church in the quadrangle with its brownstone arches surmounting greyed pillars and its background of red-tiled roofs visible under partly-thawed white snow. But the chapel, severe, plain and dimly lighted, serves for short morning and evening assemblies with their prayers and hymns and bible readings, and for longer Sunday services, as well as for less formal activities, such as choral singing. For this last, I noted, the choir master stood on one of the solid, dark old timber pews while his choristers sat about on chairs and steps and on the stone-flagged floor of the chapel entrance. The religious atmosphere is pervasive and appears in the persons of staff members, in the graces we said before and after a midday meal served in strict, almost regimented fashion, in the whole ethos of the establishment from the habitual tone of much of the instruction to the staid furnishing of staff quarters and student rooms.

What will happen to Sigtuna, and to folkhighschools like it, when almost universal education to high levels becomes the order of the Swedish 1980's?

There are many possibilities. It may be that more students than the government at present anticipates will elect to discontinue school and then resume study, even if the resumption is at a higher level than is common now. There may be an extension of "personal improvement" education on the original Danish model. There are already new and alternative models in operation: short residential courses, usually lasting from eight to eleven weeks in the June to September period, in which pensioned workers seek new interests in a wide range of adult education studies from psychology, history, and literature to craft work and folk music. Shorter discussion seminars on particular topics — nutrition or religion or peace or population — may involve a score of people for a week of more intensive work.

The demand for education that leads to greater insight and greater capacity for self-realization is unlimited and lifelong. The only purpose of the kind of so-called "education" (really "instruction") whose outcome is merely greater vocational competence is an instrumental one: to promote the economic conditions which make possible the former, wider education for human fulfilment. And this being so, Sigtuna will stand for a long time to come.

(ii) RUNÖSKOLAN

To move from Sigtuna to the folk high school at Akers-Runö is to move from one educational world to another. In the second of these on a small sea-girt wooded peninsula that it owns, TCO, the Central Organization of Salaried Employees, has established a modern outpost of a kingdom very much of this world.

Once again, in Runöskolan, one is face to face with the extraordinarily high material standards of living that so many Swedes share and take for granted. I drank coffee with the director and secretary in the folkhighschool's competely sumptuous restaurant, surrounded by the sophisticated luxury and elegant décor one finds in London's Mayfair or New York's Seventh Avenue. I commented on the contrast between this environment and the usual Western stereotype of trade union headquarters as the economically embattled headquarters of the sons of toil. My hosts looked askance — we were not communicating. "But who," I asked, waving at the subdued pastel-toned walls and ceiling, the polished timber furniture, the solid stone floors and the clustered chandeliers, "who in Sweden can afford to live in this style?" "Everybody!" they assured me, somewhat sweepingly. "Here in Sweden, we found out that it is cheaper in the long run to build well. Of course wealthy people build more space than others, but the quality doesn't change much at all." But "everybody" must wait a long time: an engaged couple may have their name on a list for years before obtaining a small flat in Stockholm. The restaurant had its space too, I noted, but made no further comment. A few minutes later our thinking was out of phase again. My economic instinct, never far below the surface, had noted with astonishment that the cost per student place in the folkhighschool (excluding the price of the land, which TCO had acquired for a mere $1 million U.S. before real estate values rocketed) was of the order of $13,000. Nobody but me was impressed. "More coffee?"

Runöskolan's few brick lodges accommodate up to 250 trades unionists for full-time study. They tend to be older than the general average for folkhighschools, some being into their thirties, a few over forty — members of the "lost generation". Some need more qualification for better positions in industry or in the trade union movement. Some may be forced to acquire new job qualifications because of accident or physical unfitness. The incentives may be social and personal as well as vocational. Some feel the need for higher education — more or less independently of the demands of the job — because they are meeting and working with others of the new generation, who have studied longer and deeper at school.

All students receive the normal State allowance, and this is generally supplemented by a scholarship from the trade union. Again, there are no examinations at the end of the course, but on request a student may obtain a report card on which he has been awarded a mark assessing his ability and knowledge in each subject. The report may be produced for a potential employer or, occasionally, as evidence of readiness for higher study.

Education, I was told, should be objective rather than indoctrinatory. The classic problem of the educator at all levels is: can it ever be? One does not doubt the goodwill of either Runöskolan or Sigtuna; yet one has a feeling that their government-sponsored, objective, non-indoctrinatory courses in history and social affairs will have a somewhat different emphasis. There are, of course, degrees of objectivity, and of indoctrination: Runöskolan students learn, amongst other things, how workers can most effectively achieve a satisfactory share of the country's increasing productivity.

Not surprisingly, formal courses at Runöskolan are biased more towards the social subjects. The range includes history, political science (national and international), economics, history of labour organization, mathematics, science, Swedish, literature, psychology. More surprisingly, to me at least, music, art and craft are not included in the regular program.

Sport, however, is strongly emphasized. In the large, gleaming timber-walled gymnasium — 60 feet wide and 120 feet long — four huge arches of laminated timber, wider than a tall man and two feet thick, rise from the timber floor's extreme limits to soar thirty feet in air and support the great curved shell of the timber ceiling and its roof. In another building, there are permanent displays on work safety and ergonomy, lighting and hearing and work study; this last practice was accepted by the Swedish trade union movement after hesitation and under careful union surveillance.

At the time of my visit, only 60 of Runöskolan's 250 places were occupied by students taking full-time (30-weeks-per-year) courses. Twenty-five of these were in first year, 20 in second, 15 in third. As in Sigtuna, other places were continuously used for short and medium-length courses lasting from a week-end up to three months.

Swedes tell me they have found a middle way between the U.S.A. and the U.S.S.R. You think of this as you walk out of the magnificent diningroom (the paintings on its walls are valued at about a quarter of a million kronor), cross the marble floors of the main hall, climb the wide, sweeping marble stairway to the luxuriously furnished group-study rooms and the lecture hall, and saunter on to the libraries and reading rooms that look out, from their airconditioned comfort, over white fields and blue sea and green forest.

The chances seem remote that even the most silver-tongued lecturer of right or left could persuade the earnest trade unionist that what Sweden urgently needs is larger industrial corporations for greater material prosperity or the dictatorship of the suffering and downtrodden proletariat.

Some tasks must daunt even the most ardent of educators.

7 Of the youth, by the youth, for the youth

Experimental Gymnasium. Norway

As this chapter is being written, the world-wide movement for youth power seems to have reached a developmental plateau. On the one hand, in most developed countries and some under-developed ones it is at least tacitly acknowledged that organized youth will remain a force to be reckoned with in social affairs, far into any foreseeable future. On the other hand, the successes of the youth movement for social and educational reform have been limited, often severely limited.

Who, in the 1970's, are the youth? None of them are over 30 and few of them are over 25. Essentially, they are the generation born after the Second World War. But at the youngest? Nineteen? Eighteen? Seventeen? Sixteen?

We know that, biologically, young people today mature into adulthood increasingly earlier than even those of two generations ago. With this biological development goes a demand for self-responsibility, an inevitable and desirable demand always, but not unlimited in its scope or its extension to lower age levels. Yet, where are the limits? In April, 1968, in the U.S.A., hundreds of thousands of students staged a one-day strike as a protest against the Vietnam involvement. In Sweden, each year, press, radio and television cover the annual conference of the high-school student movement as an event of great national importance. This pro-cedure pre-dated the three-weeks period in 1966 when (with the approval of the education authorities and the teachers' unions) the students ran the schools while the teachers were on strike. If a voteless young man of 20 — and in some cases younger — is old enough to be called up for service and possible death when his country's leaders opine that military force is the appropriate means of supporting their policy, at what stage is he mature enough to demonstrate against that policy, or to take to the barricades when his own elected youth leaders tell him that his interests as a citizen and a student are at stake? Again, if primary school democracy can mean real, effective and successful contribution to curriculum development and to disciplinary rules, as it does in Stockholm's Eiraskolan and in at least one of Denmark's progressive junior schools, how much responsibility in these areas can reasonably be entrusted to senior high school students and to the intellectual elite of university youth?

Whatever the answers to such questions, they will not be found merely in the philosophic cerebrations of the older generation, however well-intentioned, nor in the aseptic decimal-pointed research of the social scientists, however academically prestigious and meticulous. They will be wrought out in action by trial and error and trial and success.

MARCH, 1968

The Experimental Gymnasium for boys and girls aged from 16 to 18 in Oslo, Norway, stands in the poor and unlovely suburb of Toyen. It is housed in six drab, dark and unlovely rooms that were available, in a larger school, when the school year opened in September, 1967. There is little equipment; sheets of plaster board on wooden supports serve as work benches; the science facilities are off in another building. Limitations of space are frustrating to the point of agony. Meetings of large groups of the school's 137 students must jampack into classrooms that could comfortably hold 25; and nothing could exceed the courtesy far beyond the call of duty with which a longish queue of Toyen Skole's male and female students granted a visiting middle-aged Australian academic prior entry to the school's single toilet. Conditions are indeed poor by any standards in the developed world.

Yet, did I live in Oslo, I should hope my children would want to attend the school.

Toyen Skole was the brainchild of three intelligent teenagers, two boys and one girl, who decided that the education offered in Norway's senior high schools was too rigid, formalized and authoritarian, that the generation gap between the old, old-style teacher and modern youth was intolerable. "Give us a school to run." they said in effect, "and we'll show you that thorough learning and self-determination are natural allies."

The three young innovators got their school. But it was not without effort. In December of 1966 they began a public campaign that was to startle Oslo and involve most of Norway. They wrote letters to newspapers and to officials of the education ministry. They appealed for, and obtained, funds from other adolescents and from adults. They prepared and distributed circulars attacking what they said was the authoritarianism of Norwegian education; and they and others spoke to meetings of high school students urging them to support and to gather support for the idea of an experimental school.

Inevitably, some head teachers thought the circulars and the speakers, and, indeed the whole campaign, too inflammatory for their charges and refused to have either written or spoken propaganda on their premises.

On the other hand, a great many educators, authors, artists, public people, university staff (including a vice-chancellor), came out in general support of the proposal for an experimental school. Its keynotes, they said, should be co-operation and shared responsibility between staff and students rather than the authority of the former over the latter.

So youth got its school. Toyen Skole's highest administrative body is the School Council. It consists of four students, three teachers, the principal, and a representative of the Parents and Friends Association. It is this Council which has the effective power, including the power to hire and fire staff. For the record, only one teacher, to date, has been told that he wasn't fitting in and that it would be better if he sought another position elsewhere. He went.

Predictably, as keen young people and enthusiastic adults shaped and organized a campaign, the whole issue acquired political significance.

The Labour-controlled Oslo City Council was sympathetic: it made the classrooms available and promised a subsidy, since the gymnasium is not fee-paying. In the State government, whence teachers' salaries and permission to operate had to come, there was stiff opposition from some quarters.

The research people in the education department did possibly as much as anyone to clinch this particular youth victory by stating that they would like to see and co-operate in the establishment of an experimental gymnasium so that new ideas could be tried out and evaluated. In August of 1967, a month before the new school year was due to commence, the government agreed that the new institution could open with the rest of Norway's schools. Some of the school's present difficulties can reasonably be attributed to the rush to appoint staff and to organise the year's activities.

Most of this I already knew by the time I went out to Toyen Skole to talk to staff and students.

The boys and girls presently (1968) enrolled are all in the last three high school years. The head (school-leader or rektor) is Mrs. Mosse Jorgensen, and there are seven full-time teachers and 20 part-time ones. (This because the Ministry of Education gave their "blessing" too late for many teachers, who needed certain promise of a job.) As one minor but significant detail, head, staff and students address each other by christian names.

"How does it work out with the older teachers?" I enquired. "Oh, quite well," the students assured me. "It took us all two or three days to get used to the idea, and after that nobody took any notice."

According to the National Experimental Committee for Schools, Universities and High Schools, the experiment at Toyen concerns five major points: new forms of co-operation between pupils, teachers and parents; partial breaking-up of the class and timetable system to allow differentiation of work rate; extra-syllabus subjects; new teaching aids; and new examination forms. This, while it is a reasonable official paper summary, sounds pretty bloodless; and in practice both staff and students, at the heart of the affair, stress above all else the human relationships from which almost everything else flows.

While I was talking with one group of students I injudiciously made use of a phrase that I had carried over from Sweden, "student democracy". They corrected me, politely but instantaneously — "Not student democracy," they said, "school democracy. The teachers' rights are just as important as the students'."

Most of the schools I know — and I know a great many — fall into one of two categories. In the not very good ones, school is a place to which children are compelled to come and in which teachers try to compel them to learn. In the better ones, the staff have set up and retain control of an educational pattern such that it is easy for the students to work **with** their system rather than against it.

In Toyen, I felt, the ethos was different. Here students came eager to be educated — or rather to educate themselves — and they knew that teachers were there to help them when necessary. "We wanted a place," they told me, "where we could meet teachers as friends and not as masters."

The difference shows in a number of ways. No student has to attend school, for instance. If he feels he can handle a particular subject better by reading at home, he does just that. If another feels that he can do better by being demoted to an earlier class, he goes along and asks for that to be arranged. About half a dozen have done so.

Tests are regarded not as a contest between teacher and student, and not as a means of grading the latter, but as a way for both to find out what progress has been made and where more help is needed. So — and I quote from an official document — "Inspection (i.e. supervision) during these tests will of course be superfluous". There must be others, but I know of only two other institutions where tests are unsupervised: a private high school for boys in Illinois and a training college for girls in Ceylon.

I am something of a fanatic about the arrangement of desks in classrooms. If I walk along a school's corridors for two or three minutes in school hours and see — as I still see in a very large majority of classrooms — that the desks are all ranged in military rows facing the teacher, I am quite sure that I am in an educational dictatorship, however unconsciously and benevolently dictatorial it may prove to be.

In Toyen I found the desks arranged in semi-circles, in small groups, in pairs and singly. I thought this had been only a natural working-out of the philosophy of the school, but I was assured that that was not so: it was also the result of quite deliberate policy — a democratic placement of seating to reflect a democratic relationship of the people using it.

I quoted an example that I use when talking to student teachers: if you were really in egalitarian discussion with friends in your home, would you arrange the lounge chairs in formal rows and then stand up in front? The Toyen students agreed emphatically with the point of view implied.

Where, I asked, did these adolescents get their ideas on how a school should be organised? Partly they said, by reflecting on their own experience, partly by reading; in all, a pretty good formula for learning about a great many things when you look at it. Actually they surprised me with the breadth of their reading, though I hadn't time to test its depth. They knew their Paul Goodman ("Compulsory Miseducation" and "Growing Up Absurd") and they had got to know England's Dartington and Bedales schools. They were able to quote me teacher-instituted experimental schools in Denmark that I hadn't heard of. Above all, they were familiar with A. S. Neill, of course, as all young educational radicals are. "But this is **not** Summerhill," they told me firmly. "We're here because we want to pass our examinations." Thus the vocal, anyway.

More surprisingly perhaps, some had read Dewey, and at least a couple of the group had studied Theodore Brameld who argues — in "Education as Power" and "Education for the Emerging Age" — for education focused on the concept of a world civilization, and whose work is still almost unheard of by a painfully high proportion of Western educators.

The institutional bases of school democracy are the general meeting, consisting of all the students and staff, and the school council, already referred to. This general meeting, held every Friday, works up to and down from the Council, and is responsible for school discipline. "We discuss what to do about such matters as smoking," said the students, "and work and study methods, and vacations, and what machines to buy and how to organize final examinations."

I asked what would happen if all the students were in favour of some piece of policy and all the staff were opposed to it, or vice versa. They smiled and said, "It just doesn't ever work out like that; when we can't agree on something, there are always staff

and students on both sides." Nevertheless, I notice in the regulations a clause giving the unanimous staff a delaying power similar
to that of a parliamentary upper chamber.

I feel that the major fact that the Experimental Gymnasium's
still numerous opponents have to quarrel with is this: that from
Oslo and from other parts of Norway, students who had dropped
out of school came back again saying, in effect, "We still want to
learn but not the way the schools have been teaching."

It is only fair to add that there has been a counter-tide:
students left the new gymnasium of their own accord, saying it
was not for them. None, incidentally, have been asked to leave
or expelled.

I attended a lunch-hour meeting of the school Council, an
experience none the less intriguing because the whole proceedings
were conducted in Norwegian of which I do not understand a
word. Even so, some highly significant things came through. A
couple of council members explained to me, in English, the business of the meeting. Some of the students had been studying
Russian and Spanish, not because they are on the examination
syllabus (they aren't) but because they wanted to learn Russian
and Spanish. Now one member of staff had drafted a letter to the
authorities asking that these two languages be examined for credit,
and the council was trying to ensure that the case was put as
fully, clearly and convincingly as possible.

In the absence of the rektor, this meeting was chaired by a
young man who was either a very self-assured and mature student
or a very young teacher. It didn't occur to me to enquire which,
and nothing in what the discussion revealed of interpersonal
relationships round the table could possibly help the uninitiated
visitor to decide.

Of course the experimental gymnasium is not an idyllic educational paradise with all its questions answered and all its difficulties ironed out. It is, (i.e. it was when I wrote this) after all,
less than a year old. "We're still working things out, learning
how to work together," they assured me. And of course there are
plenty of problems.

Naturally the school wants its own building. The present
premises are not only spatially inadequate but, as I have suggested, stark and decrepit. This is so, even though the students
have brightened them up by putting huge abstracts and other
artwork on walls and blackboards— a procedure frowned upon,
they tell me, by a very conservative inspector who felt that blackboards are for writing on, not for decorating, just as desks out
of place and students sitting in corridors were also Bad Things.
Staff and students feel that not nearly enough experimentation is
going on, especially with new subjects and new examination
techniques; and they are annoyed when the value of the school

is called into question, on the basis of its paucity of experimental work, by people whose business it is to expedite that work. There is a great shortage of equipment, more permanent teachers are needed, and so on.

And there are the personal and social problems — the young idealists torn between helping to save the world now, in Vietnam, Africa and elsewhere, and, alternatively, educating themselves to a point where they will be better saviours in the future. Some parents assent only reluctantly to their children's attendance here. I made an informed guess at what might be some of the vital statistics for a group of one hundred and fifty Australian sixteen-to-eighteen-year-olds in a similar situation, how many would be smoking, drinking, using drugs, cohabiting. "We have no statistics," said the students, but they did not feel obliged to express any alarm or denials, perhaps because my estimates were fairly low by world standards.

Again, while many of the students felt (and none disagreed) that the new atmosphere had developed a camaraderie, absent in other schools, that cut clean across the dividing lines between first, second and third year students, some at least voiced an uneasy conviction that there was a tendency for exclusive groups to form within the total student body. "There are too many outsiders," said one blonde Norwegian girl.

What is the likely future of the experimental gymnasium? The intention is to expand the enrolment from its present one hundred and forty to two hundred and fifty or perhaps more — but not very many more, since there is a belief that unity and partici-patory democracy depend on small numbers. The young lady who helped found the school — her name is Ingrid Kviberg — hopes for an experimental democratic primary school on modified lines, but feels that the time for it will not be ripe for a few years.

Meanwhile, the continuation of the experiment is by no means certain. There remains opposition. Not, I gathered, from the majority of members of the Teachers Union — who are popularly supposed to be antagonistic. The thing they couldn't stomach was — and is — year-by-year appointment, and that by a strongly student-influenced council, in a profession that traditionally offers lifetime security.

Rather, the doubts are at the political level. I asked the students, "What would you do if the school had to close because it received no more finance?" Most, though not all, said they would go on studying in another school, but reluctantly. Generally, they would be unhappy, but after the experience of Toyen they would know how to educate themselves — if necessary in spite of the school. One added that she would go to another school but under protest, and another said she would do so to make a revolution. Pedagogues of all lands — or of Norway anyhow — had better unite. Already student organizations in other high schools, encouraged by the gymnasium's example, are calling for representation at staff meetings.

What does it all add up to? The process of becoming a self-determining adult in a fully democratic society must necessarily involve learning to make increasingly important responsible choices in one's earlier living; and not many schools — or many homes either — are conspicuously successful in allowing and encouraging children and adolescents to make responsible choices about important matters.

Where are the limits? They are certainly different at different times and in different cultures. It will take a great many Toyen Skoles to find out.

Footnote.

6th December, 1968

Dear Mr. Schoenheimer,

Thank you for sending us the draft of your chapter on us. I must apologise for not answering your letter earlier, but I'm sure you understand how things are.

As you say in your letter, you are trying to give your impressions of our school at the time you were there, and this makes it difficult for me to refrain from sending you a new extra chapter. I have, however, in case you wanted to make use of it, sent a supplement with the next instalment of what at times seems like a combination of all the detective stories written. A **final** chapter is always an anti-climax.

It was also a little strange reading about "us-last-year". Like looking at an old photograph where we can pick out a few well-known traits. And now there are so many new faces in the picture. The final chapter if it was ever written would have to be: "We've closed".

Let me just then wish you luck with the whole enterprise. Maybe we could even see the finished work?

Yours very sincerely,

Mosse Jorgensen.

Since last year certain changes have taken place.

The biggest of all perhaps: we have moved.

The building we have moved into is one which once upon a time was the Headmaster's house of the first Cathedral school in Oslo. Instead of long institution-like corridors we now have hallways, dark staircases and lots of small corners where clothes and papers and bags and books can happily collect: to the despair of our weekly clearance group. We also have a small kitchen. Our long-suffering secretary has now got a small office nearly all for herself, which for some reason or other she wanted painted in sterile white. Her wish was granted and she added a few rays of sunshine with shelves of brilliant yellow.

The other rooms are different.

We have also got what we dreamt about all last year when we sat and smoked and chatted in the dark corridors at Toyen. A beautiful big room for us all to relax in.

The big room has lots of large windows which we have adorned with modern curtaining. We have bought some light-wooded round tables and attractive red chairs. New lamps. New monster of a cola-machine. And trouble. The music lovers want quiet. The studious want a work-and-discussion room. The smokers smoke (the only room the Fire authorities allow smoking in the building). The non-smokers want a half-an-hour break from smoke — with fresh air. Some feel too many play too much chess. Some feel too many play cards too much. Some just feel — quietly. Some just complain. It's a room where everyone can go — but relax . . . well.

Many of our teaching experiments (that is inside the different subjects) which we have sent the Ministry of Education for their acceptance, we have not yet received an answer to. But we are trying them out anyway. We are now in the middle of discussions for our pedagogical lay-out for 1969/70. It promises to be interesting. — M.J.

8 Now, in Ardwick, green grass grows

Primary School. England

In most education systems of the developed world there is a seeming contradiction that bears pondering on. On the one hand, the custom is to demand higher levels of intellectual attainment and a longer period of preparation for potential secondary school teachers; on the other hand, it is in the primary (or elementary) schools that one usually finds most vitality and innovation.

There are at least two principal explanations of this situation. The child in pre-school and infant classes still relates very closely to the home, and the school is seen as an extension of the home, which is a human and humane institution. The higher up the educational ladder he goes, the closer he comes to the impersonality of the adult world of employment and the marketplace, and, consequently, the longer and darker are the shadows that these inhumane entities throw into the classroom. In the early years, the temporal and spatial proximity of love and affection and the relatively long distance before economic pressure for job training combine to allow the infant a breathing space when he may be educated as an individual and a person, excitingly, considerately, joyfully — the only way effective learning happens.

Gradually at best, and sometimes all too rapidly, he is transformed into a unit being force-filled on an instructional belt-line that will deliver him, a standard-shaped, well-fitting mass-processed product, to the alienation of the factory and the anomie of suburbia. Rightly or wrongly (and, the sociologists are beginning to suggest, short-sightedly), the iron hands of commerce and industry have not yet reached down into the kindergarten. The machine has allowed the luxury of humanization to the pre-school.

The second factor is the obverse of the first. The primary school teacher, it was believed (wrongly, as events are showing, but let that pass) needed less understanding of academic subjects.

She was therefore able, even in a shorter training course, to devote more time than her secondary colleague to professional preparation in the human art of pedagogy. She may have been a lesser scholar, but she could be a better teacher. Even today, in highly developed countries, it is common for a degree-holding secondary-school teacher to have spent only one year of a four-year course in professional as distinct from academic preparation, while a primary teacher will have devoted a year-and-a-half or more of a three-year course to pedagogical training.

So it is that most secondary schools tend to change the content of their curricula far more than the general nature of the educational (or instructional) experience they offer; whereas a far larger proportion of primary schools are open to vital reconstructions. . . .

Now, in the suburb of Ardwick, in black and grimy industrial Manchester, U.K., for a century no grass grew. And on summer evenings, mothers and fathers would go with their children a mile or so, that they might see green grass and walk on it and roll in it — much in the way that parents in other cities take their off-spring in the family car to the country or the seaside.

And in Armitage Street, in the heart of this urban desert, among a redevelopment plan that is replacing the unlovely century-old slum houses and slum warehouses, stands the Armitage School, beautiful with glass and timber and stone — and grass.

By traditional standards — the standards that applied when most readers of this book were in primary grades — Armitage is a strange school. If you walk into the nursery or infant section on an average morning, no child will be sitting in his place, because no child **has** a place. If you ask what lesson it is, nobody will be able to tell you, because it isn't any particular lesson. And you will look in vain for the teacher who is teaching the class, because that is not the teacher's task.

What you will find going on, however, is just about as much self-directed **learning** as ever went on in any equal area of school-space.

Likely, there will be, among the infants (aged from 5 to 7), in one place, a group of eight or ten all working at different number "games", colouring or counting, sorting number trays, manipulating number blocks, or weighing beans in one pan against an eraser in another and recording the findings; another group may be reading in the "quiet area" from word-and-picture charts, or reading cards, or simple books; and yet another will be busy at tables in the window bay, copying stories or writing their own. Six or eight of the class are standing in file at the teacher's table, waiting their turn for work to be checked or questions answered or assistance given.

Armitage was built as a pace-setter school for just this kind of learning. The methods in use are advanced, but, in the U.K., a long way from unique. The building, however, is avant-garde.

The school is designed to hold 310 students aged from 3½ years to eleven. Not only does the child not have a particular place in a room; it is at least partly true to say that he does not have a room either, though he does have the security of a home base.

From a central hall, the school radiates into four asymmetrical wings. Each wing includes the home learning space of some 80 children — two year-groups that make a loose federation. Children regard themselves as basically members of one or other group; but they move freely between the two; and the two teachers exchange posts at agreed times for an hour or a morning, so that there is a variety of personal contact.

It is impossible to overstress the importance of Armitage County School's architecture. The general plan is to provide four activity areas for each group of 40 pupils. If you want to talk of a "classroom", these four areas inside a basic rectangle constitute it.

The first is a dining, reading and writing area, a large bay with space for sixteen at the window seats, tables and chairs. At lunch-time, books are moved to nearby shelves and places are set beneath the low pendant lights.

The main Work Area is as large as a normal class-room (540 square feet). In it, children may be gathered together for a class activity, or they may work in small groups operating round movable tables which, with their attendant chairs, can be rapidly rearranged.

A craft or utility area, equipped where necessary with taps, electric points and benches, is lightly screened from the main Work Area. It opens to paved outside space.

Finally there is the alcove, a kind of small sitting room for quiet study or reading or story-telling, with or without a teacher. Carpeted and curtained off, set with window seats, window curtains, pendant lights and a few tables and upholstered chairs, it provides a variation of atmosphere for a different kind of learning situation.

This, then is the basic architectural pattern, repeated eight times with slight modifications, for the different age groups. It is a pattern not merely in harmony with the changed emphasis from teaching to learning. It presupposes such a change. Ultimately, a sufficiently unsympathetic teacher could over-ride it and impose an authoritarian room atmosphere, just as a humane teacher can overcome to a large extent the rigidity inherent in the typical egg-crate classroom; for human relationships are basic. Yet in each case the physical layout exerts a powerful influence.

For the statistically-minded, each double classroom unit contains approximately 2,000 square feet of indoor space — say, 25 square feet per child. This is approximately twice the legal minimum. The hall contains another 1,800 square feet.

Hand-in-hand with any architectural concept in education goes a furnishing one. The traditional too-small, too-heavy double desk, still sometimes screwed to the floor, reflects a view of education as passive instruction for which the essential furnishing need was space to sit on, space to write on, and space to store books and materials; in each case, the minimum of space at the lowest possible cost. Such desks are not only a hindrance to real education; as a legacy of this limited kind of thinking, and of lack of concern for the welfare of the individual child, even in the world's wealthy industrialized nations (considered as a group) the majority of schoolchildren are still compelled to adopt sitting positions that, in addition to carrying a greater or lesser risk of future postural problems, must interfere with full concentration.

Furniture in Armitage Street was evolved, after much research, for a consortium of local authorities in education. Its keynotes are function, flexibility and attractiveness.

Desks, as we know them, are gone. In any one room, chairs and tables are of varying heights. Tables vary in shape. Some are circular, some square, some trapezoidal, some rectangular. Each trapezoid is half a hexagon, so that when a group of six want to confer they do so at a six-sided table made from two smaller ones. For a group of eight, a rectangle fits, as it is designed to do, between the two trapezoids, to convert the hexagon to an octagon. If even larger groups are needed, they make an ⌞ or a ⌐⌐ out of rectangles.

Strategically placed to allow plenty of passageway, these tables (with their trays of learning materials in the lower classes) break up the one main Work Area into a number of smaller ones. Their tops are linoleum-covered in varying but harmonizing colours. Linoleum is a good wearing surface, easily cleaned, suitable for both writing and eating, and far quieter than timber. Chair backs also are part of the colour harmony.

Other furniture includes mobile trolleys for books and equipment, display units, bookshelves, and workbenches. In the "classrooms", blackboards have been replaced by plain-surfaced linoboards. In the hall, furniture is collapsible or stackable or both. Amongst the furnishings are modern light fittings, carefully related to and harmonizing with the direct overhead lighting and light timber rafters, and vinyl-tiled floors. The local education authority has agreed that the standard issue of two pianos does not meet the needs of 310 children and has provided a third.

As I have indicated elsewhere in this book, I am as aware of the economics of education as most people. Good education is expensive and will always be so because its chief ingredient is highly-qualified teachers.

But function and flexibility and beauty of school buildings and furniture are not costly by any standards applicable to a modern society. They demand thought, concern, initiative, professional insight. Armitage School building, which has the qualities all children should find in their surroundings, cost £204 plus a few shillings per place to build; if it is completely demolished in twenty years' time, it will have cost the quite insignificant sum of £10 per child per year — four shillings per week. Actually its life expectancy is much nearer to 40 years than 20. (The old school, demolished to make way for Armitage, was built in 1877.) The whole of the furniture, tasteful, pleasing and completely suited to its purposes, cost £9,300 or £30 per place. If it is all burnt or thrown away at the end of thirteen years — a time arrived at by allowing the statutory $7\frac{1}{2}\%$ per annum for depreciation — it will have cost a shade less than a shilling a week per child. It is statistics of this kind that bring tears to the eyes or fury to the heart of the educational reformer in every country when he sees children herded cheek-by-jowl at poky little ugly desks in jampacked little ugly classrooms, neither desks nor rooms healthy or functional, and each having cost as much or almost as much as intelligently-designed counterparts.

It is apparent that the key concept of all of Armitage School's activities is flexibility. The rigidly furnished old-style classroom with its rigid furniture and rigid spatial relationships, is matched by a similar rigidity in relation to time and movement and subject matter. This thirty minutes is for English, that thirty-five for mathematics. Each week is a repetition of the last, each pupil moves from one room to the next on the same date.

In Armitage there is a maximum of flexibility in all these aspects. Indeed, they are part of a whole, each implying the other, and it would be wrong to regard any one of them as basic. If a child is moving through his studies at his own pace rather than in time with a class lock-step, it logically follows that he will move to the next section of the school at the time most appropriate to him. So, in September, when the new school year begins, only about eight or ten of the school's pupils will be changing from the infant wing to the first juniors (7-9), and from the first juniors to the second juniors (9-11) and so on, giving the teacher, as a bonus, only that number of new faces and new individual attainment patterns to learn. Another eight or ten came in July, there will be more in January and early April.

Timetables in the school last for four weeks or so. They are skeletal and variable, concerned mainly with the sharing of the hall, with combined class programs and broad-pattern time allocations. Thus a Tuesday timetable in the infant section may say,

"A.M. Junior Assembly, 5's to Miss G., 6's to Miss B., **3R activi-**ties, Children's Own Choice. P.M. Music, 6's to Miss L., 5's to Miss G.; Story, Poetry, Speech Rhymes." Nobody stops an activity **merely** because the hands of the clock are in a certain position, nor does he continue with it **merely** because they haven't arrived there yet.

There are now three "integrated" afternoons every week, when teachers from different levels move to various wings of the school, working in those areas where they have special interest and competence: creative drama, art and craft, French (from age 7), and physical education were examples at the time of my visit. No doubt, with different teachers having different strengths, these have changed now.

Whatever the children may be learning as what the communications experts call "in-put", is related as actively as possible to "output", which may be in the form of speech, writing, art or drama. A number of paintings of vases with leaves in them had statements written beneath. Thus Kevin (age 7) had written "the vase is made out of metal and it looks like gold and it looks like the sun" and Paul (also 7) had titled his effort **Jar of Twiggs.** "The jar is made of metal and it looks like brass, copper, gold and bronss and you could see your face in it the twiggs have buds are like beans and the twigs are brown and there are some puse-willow." English? Art? Nature Study? Science? Or simply education?

By the time they reach the higher grades, the pupils are ready to work in a structure that has rather more definition to it, though it is still far closer to the ethos of the lower classes of the school than to the traditional teacher-dominated one. Throughout the school six aspects of study are distinguished in theory and for planning purposes, but they merge and overlap in practice. These are: **basic techniques** of English and number; **creative work** in writing, drama, art and craft and (interestingly) physical education; **enlargement of the environment** including a second language; **explanation of the universe** — science, geography, social studies, **heritage of the past**; and **general — physical activity.**

Over the primary school years these strands become more distinguishable, and, although basic skills are still studied individually, there is much more likelihood that a class, as individuals or divided into groups, will all be working in one broad area at the same time; or coming together to report their findings from field or library research; or working out a large-scale project that involves the whole class.

The Nuffield Curriculum Guides are being used, experimentally, with the highest class. This is very much a working-class community group of children, the highest reading age being 12. (In any country, many children of 11-plus have a "reading age" of 14 or higher.) Yet its science course includes such topics as friction, surveying, relative weights (specific), gears, sound, optics, gravity, displacement, and kinds of energy. Mathematics seeks for: ability to quote relevant mathematical laws; ability to make statements about sets of numbers; the concept of function; knowledge of directed numbers; concept of (a number) base; understanding of closure and commutation; loci; knowledge of centre of gravity of regular and irregular shapes. These children also study histograms and topology and introductory algebra.

I saw, too, a reporting session in social studies. The treatment was fairly standard for this learning area. A number of leader-organized groups had made broad-scale co-operative investigations of countries in which they were interested. I noted with some satisfaction that along with Japan and South Africa and others Australia had been selected. The country had been researched in a number of aspects, maps had been drawn, reports written, charts of pictures and drawings prepared. Now each group was presenting its findings, verbally and pictorially, to the class, each member of the group adding his contribution to round out the full account.

In the hall, I passed, at one stage, the creation of an unscripted drama related to study of an historical topic. A thief, captured in the market-place, was being haled — pretty unceremoniously — before a judge and jury. "What is the charge?" enquired the judge. Voices erupted. Nobody quite seemed to know who ought to answer such a question so the prisoner decided to explain. The teacher intervened to assist in getting more realism. A little while later I happened to pass through the hall again. Order was now established. "What is your verdict?" enquired his honour, gravely; and the foreman of the jury replied, with equal gravity, "Unanimous!"

The emphasis on learning rather than on teaching is, of course, more than a way of getting schoolwork done. It is that, indeed. With thirty years of experience in primary and secondary school behind me, I looked in vain for the children in Armitage who were wasting time or preventing their neighbours from working. But the real outcome is the development of self-responsibility, the acceptance of the task as one's own. Children are interested in learning. They set themselves their own challenges, as anyone can see who has watched them add increasing difficulty to ball and rope games as soon as their skill and co-ordination are more than equal to an earlier stage. In games, the guidance comes from older children whose role, accepted unconsciously, is simply to show what the future stages of development can be. Inside the school, the teacher accepts this role, a more exacting and arduous one, since the intellectual, social and emotional education she is concerned with are so much wider and more complex than the simple informal games-skills education of the playground.

The term "match" has acquired a technical significance in

education. It refers to the need for the new experiences offered to the child to be neither so difficult that he is discouraged from attempting them nor so easy that he gains nothing from them. So teachers in the new primary school would like smaller classes, not because of the disciplinary problems involved in "controlling" 40 children (the authoritarian teacher's perpetual worry), but because of the difficulty of keeping abreast of each of the many and varying needs of each of many and varying children, each one growing at his own pace.

It is an entirely new approach to teaching compared with that of a generation ago when, inside a few minutes, the teacher may have read one seven-year-old's writing and discussed it with him; suggested that he can now move on to work with a number tray; proposed to another that he might put some numbers into his pictures; and gently but firmly enquired of a third when he is going to put away his colouring and do some word games. It is a different disciplinary situation from that of the old-fashioned classroom autocrat when another teacher, noticing a small group of five- and six-year-olds sitting quietly at a table with coloured paper for pasting but with no glue says quietly, "Those who have their material could go and get some glue," and adds, sotto voce, to me, "No initiative, so many children in these younger groups. They don't think for themselves. They wait for me to tell them what to do."

A seven-year-old ruled a firm black vertical line to split her blank white page in halves, then placed her ruler on the desk in front of her and went on lettering. A few seconds later she tsk-tsk-ed, got up, and put the ruler back tidily in the ruler box. Her line was obviously ten degrees off vertical. Nobody told her it was wrong or made her rub it out. It served her purpose, at her seven-year level. At eight or nine or at seven-plus-a-little-more, she would set herself a higher standard and either figure out a way to put a midway marker point at top and bottom of the page, or get the idea from a companion, or ask the teacher.

An insignificant detail? My artistic soul still carries the scars got by unhappily rubbing red marks onto just such white paper so that my lines and ellipses might meet the teacher's purposes, which were those of the inspector, which were those of the set curriculum, which were those — presumably — of God. **(Syllabus for third week: horizontal and vertical lines; bisecting a page in each direction. Amen!)**

There are no real divisions between individual and social development — it is the individual IN society who develops. So the Armitage School pupil who is learning to use the library effectively is developing his individual study skills; but before he leaves the school he is expected to have become quite proficient in acting as librarian for the rest of his group. Again, at mealtimes, a senior boy and girl are host and hostess to the other six at their lunch table, acquiring social skills in and through social activity.

No professional teacher who has read thus far is likely to be asking, "But what about discipline?" Discipline is not a way of imposing order on children so that instruction may begin or continue. Discipline (its derivation is the same as that of "disciple") is merely an aspect of the way the process of education is carried on. When a teacher knows how to co-operate with children in their natural desire to learn, **that** is his way of maintaining discipline; if he doesn't, the best he can hope for is order. Like ethics, discipline is not something extraneous, but something inherent in the school ethos and the social climate of the classroom.

None of this is to deny that Armitage Street still has some disciplinary problems. The most serious offence is usually bullying, and here the head acts quite firmly on behalf of the school code, even to the extent, on very rare occasions, of reverting to corporal punishment.

There are rewards too. Armitage awards little medals for a 90% average or better — four colours of medals for the last four years. And 100% attendance (with special provision for those accompanying parents away at the time of father's vacation) earns a book prize. I was not happy with these little bits of extrinsic motivation, even though the children sported their medals proudly enough.

What were the special circumstances afforded this experimental school? None, apart from its building, furnishing and approach. The staff were not hand-picked, nor were materials provided for which other schools must wait. The head teacher, Mr. Batson (who teachers for 60% of his time), felt that the point of the exercise was to show that the school could grow naturally with no particular advantages.

"How long," I enquired of an infant teacher, "would it take for somebody like myself, interested, sympathetic to progressive ideas, and experienced in more formal primary education, to learn to succeed with the flexible and individual methods of Armitage?" She thought perhaps eighteen months. For the first term the new teacher was lost, by the end of the first year she could see signs of progress. She instanced three teachers in their sixties, able, old-fashioned bodies, trained 40 years earlier, but dedicated and willing to try anything that could help children. All were eventually highly successful, the most capable retiring, delighted and rejuvenated, at seventy-one.

Mr. Batson was not happy with the transfer of children at eleven-plus to a new school. He felt that they should go through the storm and stress years of early puberty, say to age 13, in an environment where they were known and understood and could feel secure. Well . . . yes. But puberty gives way to middle adolescence, itself by no means an easy time in Western cultures, and there is no age between 3 and 20 when children and young people, in one developed country or another, are not commencing to learn in a new pre-school or school or college or university.

A generation ago, the more radical progressive educationists looked to the school as a focal point from which society might be reformed. Society has proved itself more resilient than they hoped, and progress must move on many fronts, of which the school is but one. Yet this being said, there is social significance in the fact of Armitage. Many of its pupils come from homes where life is depressing, unstimulating, unlovely, mean and poor. Afternoons, they leave school (which has itself a bare three acres) to play their football on a cindertip in the shadow of drab warehouses and chimneys that assail eye and nose with the depressing heritage of the Industrial Revolution.

Into the bleakness that is suburban Manchester an imaginative planning authority is letting new light — replacing aged, ugly, unfit buildings with modern flats and maisonettes, and adding Armitage County Primary School for good measure. If a beneficent contagion brings a higher quality of living through the town and its environs, nobody will be able to measure the school's influence and put in the decimal points. And yet it will be there, as certain and intangible as the influence of devoted nursing in the haleness of a once-ill child.

That is one of the things that education is all about.

9 The pursuit of excellence

(i) Bronx High School of Science. USA

Extra-corporal Extraventricular Cardiac Prosthesis; Design of a Low Band-width System of Phase Modulated Synchronized Subcarrier Cathode Ray Facsimile; Fortran Mast—a New Process of the IBM 1620.

Now what are all those about? They are typical reports of special projects designed and undertaken by bright senior students of the Bronx High School of Science, New York.

American Foreign Policy and the Revolutionary Ethics; Petain: A Hollow Hero; Pan-Africanism and Kwami Nkruhmah.

Those were three of a dozen articles published in the June, 1966 Social Studies Journal of the Bronx High School of Science.

Bite, Damned Sea; The Funeral of the Snow; In Oils Exposed; A Scattering of Petals . . . titles of pieces from the 1966 issue of Dynamo, literary magazine of the Bronx High School of Science. . . .

New York city with a population of twelve millions has precisely five schools for the especially talented: Stuyvesant, an academic high school for boys; Brooklyn Technical High School for future engineers; the High School of Music and Art; the High School of the Performing Arts (Dance and Drama); and the Bronx High School of Science.

Round the world, few educational battles rage as fiercely as those for and against schools for the gifted. The terrain itself is uncertain. Nobody greatly objects to special schools for those showing great artistic promise. Clearly, the government schools of most, perhaps all, countries are not equipped to enable them to develop their full potential; and the artists are not going to become a ruling meritocracy — not in the next decade or two, to be sure. But what of the scientific elite? Is there some danger

71

in educating them apart from their less gifted fellows? Are they an intellectual cream who need the democratic ethos of the comprehensive high school to keep them from losing the common touch? Can they reach the limits of their potential without the same kind of considered attention to their special needs as most developed societies already extend to those at the other end of the academic scale? What are the democratic rights of the brilliant?

If we had definitive answers to any or all of these questions, the heat would go out of the debate around special schools.

Meanwhile, the Bronx High School of Science, in its fourth decade, goes on pouring out close to a thousand high-school graduates each year, bound, without exception, for college or university. Eighty per cent of them are scholarship winners. In due course, alumni have become professors, renowned scientists, key personnel in research and development. Whatever the merits or demerits of its **raison d'etre**, BHSS remains, at its level, one of the intellectual power-houses of the USA.

This is a large school, with some 3,000 students. There is a single entry qualification: merit. Each year, a highly select group of about four thousand junior high school students from New York City sit the stiff entrance examinations. Of these, about a quarter gain admission on the basis of their examination results, previous academic records, special attainments, and lower-school achievements.

The resulting intake average about one year younger than their peers in other schools and about two years ahead of them in literacy and numeracy, as well as having pronounced ability in science and mathematics. If high school is becoming a rat race, these are Derby rats — 1800 male to 1200 female; which proportions, I am told, seem to represent fairly well the sexual spread of scientific talent.

Typically, the U.S. student entering a senior high school expects an extremely wide range of study options. In BHSS he does not get them. "The school takes the view," says its principal, Dr. Alexander Taffel, "that the faculty knows better than the student at this early stage of his life what combinations of courses will provide a sound educational base."

So most of the student's program is prescribed; but the prescription is not narrowly scientific and mathematical. Indeed, its main aim is to make such ultra-specialization impossible.

During the four years of his course, every student is required to study: 4 years of English; 4 years of Social Studies (BHSS believes that it is probably the only U.S. high school with this particular stipulation); 4 years of science; 3 or 4 years of one foreign language; 3 years of mathematics. Other required subjects, not to nearly so high a level, include mechanical drawing, science techniques laboratory (involving practical constructive work with wood, metals, plastic, glass and so on), music, health education, and art education. One-year selective courses still leave the student opportunity to pursue interests from electronics to field biology and from linear programming to nutrition or the history and development of science.

In the fairly standard USA high-school pattern, there are Advanced (College-level) courses which overlap the normal work of freshman-year in the higher institution. Each student of BHSS must take two such advanced courses. Expectedly, the preponderant choices are in the sciences and mathematics. But there are College-level literature, history and language courses, and the school has so many highly talented artists that it offers advanced art as a subject.

Most of the normal school problems of "discipline" are non-existent or almost so in BHSS. They have been obviated rather than solved. Too many controls are operating, in the very nature of the situation. The children's presence rests on the twin bases of interest and ability. "Failure" is at worst only relative. Even the student who is "failing" in the competitive sense within the school has the compensation of knowing that he is succeeding by all other criteria. And at the same time the competition remains as a significant control.

Behind the in-school situation is the parental attitude, strongly supportive and also competitive. In a city where 50% of the school population is of Negro or Puerto Rican origin, these two groups are a very small minority of the Bronx High School of Science: not on any grounds of principle or theory, of course, but, pragmatically, because, by the age of entry to high school, comparatively few such children have reached the required level for admission to the school. The school population leans perhaps a little more to the upwardly striving lower middle class than to the upper middle. I sought statistics on the Jewish population, knowing, by my own upbringing and five years of teaching in a prestigious Jewish school, how ardently Jewish parents seek intellectual excellence for their children. The statistics were not available — did not exist. Once the school had had a highly concentrated Jewish population; and although there had been a change due to the Great Population Drift of the block-busting desegregation era, it is conceivable that a majority of the students are Jewish still. In any case, Jewish or not, there is a uniquely representative parent body that draws in at least one member of almost every family, is extremely active in school affairs, and cannot but reflect a powerful parental influence towards diligence and co-operativeness in school work.

With all these forces at work, there are only the very rarest of occurrences of truancy, lateness, indiscipline in its usual senses. I sat in on a couple of Sociology lessons which ran along capably and semi-formally, with the teacher conducting a modified exposition-demonstration-discussion that would have seemed rather dull and uninspiring to students of average and below-average ability, but which were neither of these things in the context. Students were with and ahead of the teacher all the way, questions elicited intelligent and interesting sidelights and insights beyond the competence of any one mortal teacher as different boys and girls of each group's 30-odd added their meed of enlightenment to the group experiences. One of the lessons, incidentally (for which I arrived half-way through) had either started as physiology and veered off into sex education, or started as sex education and gone physiological. In any event it was treated as one more interesting and serious extension of understanding, and the smiles that greeted one unintentional risque remark by a bright sixteen-year-old girl had much of the amused indulgence of intelligent adults and no hint at all of sniggering.

Before and behind the class lesson is a lot of assigned reading which, in the circumstances, a teacher can assume will be completed and understood. This is not the high-school norm. Like most students, those of Bronx High complain of heavy demands on their time; but here the work gets done.

Nevertheless, in spite of the highly co-operative classroom atmosphere, or perhaps because of it and by way of reaction, there are other problems. One was identified for me as the malaise of the era, alienation — rebellion without a cause, rejection without a program, a refusal of what is without an idea of what should be. "Protest" and "having our share" are the watchwords, and "our share" includes experimentation with marijuana and LSD, while "protest" opposes regulations concerning the external bugbears of uniforms and haircuts.

Since my personal interests are in the arts and humanities rather than the sciences, I looked for evidence of their state of health. As with art, so with music, there are many highly gifted individuals. There are a strong school orchestra and a school choir, as well as individuals and groups who perform informally and learn, but not for examination credit. Interestingly, the chairman of the music department takes mathematics classes in the evenings.

Most BHSS male students, after having won bushels of awards in national science talent quests, finish up in some field of science or engineering, and many of the girls go on to teach in high schools or colleges. Only a very few become outstanding in other fields. The school's classes in journalism, literature and creative writing presumably contributed to the successes of alumni like Peter Beagle, author of two novels and one book of travel; another who recently won a $1000-dollar prize for a novel and one negro author, who is living in Greenwich Village and making a quite remunerative best of both worlds by writing science fiction.

How "democratic" is the Bronx High School of Science? It

depends what you mean by the term. Is exclusiveness on **any** basis automatically undemocratic? The school admits each year 100 students (10% of its intake) on the basis that though they are really below the borderline for acceptance, their junior high school principals have certified that home and other conditions of under-privilege have militated against them. They tend to survive in the bottom quarter of their classes. Again, the students are respon-sible for a good deal of community service, helping to support hospitals, charities, neighbourhood play areas. "Intellectual snob-bery?" "No chance of it," I was told, "when every person in the room knows more than you do about some things."

More persistent than these side issues are the perennial matters. Is a democracy better off, in the long run, if the members of its intellectual elite are given special opportunities to develop all their potential excellence? Come the millenium, everybody will receive a magnificent all-round fully satisfying and deeply humanizing education; but what of here, now, today, with the current enemy (whoever he may be by the time this is published) pushing ahead with research and the cultivation of highly speci-alized talent? Given the present state of the schools, how true is it that it is the brilliant who tend to get lost in the shuffle? And how much does that matter ultimately, to them and the com-munity? Those of us who have taught at tertiary levels in the decades of the education explosion are familiar with the not in-considerable group of high-ability students who have succeeded so well in relation to their fellows with so little effort that they quite literally do not realize just how much more they are capable of if they are challenged to achieve not a grade or a place but their own best.

It doesn't happen at the Bronx High School of Science.

(ii) Dalton School. USA

Every Western teacher and student teacher has heard of the Dalton Plan: when it stopped being an aspect of methodology it became part of educational history.

The Dalton School was founded in 1919 by Helen Parkhurst, a progressive educational reformer. Its distinguishing feature was its system of "contracts" or assignments which allowed each child to "contract" to complete a certain amount of work by a given time, moving at his own optimum pace rather than being hustled uncomprehendingly along or dragged boringly back to match the lock-step of formal class teaching.

Today, Dalton School remains independent, co-educational, academic, expensive. Individualized study methods are still an integral part of its program; but under its present headmaster, Donald Barr, they are woven into a very different fabric from that of the easygoing, extremely child-centred place that the school had become by the fifties and sixties.

Barr would object almost as strongly to being called anti-progressive in the general sense as he would to being labelled a "progressive" in the ultra-permissive connotation of the term. A product of present USA and its problems, he is opposed to these neo-Freudians who object to all controls and all repression of children's urges, opposed to the over-permissiveness which he identifies with social and moral slackness and lack of guts on the part of parents and teachers.

"Fundamentally," he says, "children need to be in the presence of adults who believe in their culture with calm, confident zest and who exercise authority but with respect for the individual." And, correlatively, "The curriculum has its own integrity. It is the racial heritage. This does not mean that a lesson should be planned ahead in detail, as too many of the old-style teachers like to believe. It is possible to combine respect for the integrity of academic material with a very flexible handling of the child's meeting with that material."

Until they are translated into practice, such statements are apt to remain somewhat unreal. But in Dalton School, practice follows precept.

One example that illustrates the thesis is the teaching of high school English. A student is free to choose from a wide range (seventeen in all) of different reading assignment courses, some lasting for one semester, some for two. The options are not soft: typical would be: Major British Novelists, Major American Poets, Shakespearean Tragedy, Greek Drama. And the treatment is deep and scholarly, much more so than in most high school courses.

Yet the choice is real. The racial heritage is rich enough, Barr insists, that a student can even afford to omit Shakespeare, and Milton too, without fatal consequences. No single author or area is quintessential. What is vital is that he must have read much of the best poetry and drama and know how to read both poems and plays. The assignments see to it that this objective is achieved, and that prose, too, gets its share of attention.

So, if the student can persuade his house advisor that the course he has selected is a good one for him, he is usually allowed to proceed. In practice, I was assured, there are very few vetoes on student choices.

Study methods are of four kinds. A normal assignment frequently begins with one or more sessions or class "conferences" at which a plan of attack is discussed. This is followed by reading, reference and writing at home and in laboratory periods; some of these are partly tutorial in nature, some are purely private study except that a teacher is available for consultation. In due course, the developments lead back to further discussion and evaluation in class, commencing a new cycle of inquiry. It is "inquiry", in Barr's eyes, which focuses the learning process.

But the outcome of the inquiry still leaves a wide range of option to the student. If he is studying Milton, for example, he may elect to write any one of a large number of essays; or he may prefer to produce a 30-line or 40-line Miltonic invocation to an (imaginary) epic of his own; or he may propose some other creative response to the material he has been engaged on. Other things being equal or nearly so, an original response is always preferred.

It is this balance between authority and initiative, structure and freedom, material and treatment, subject and student, that Dalton seeks to maintain.

$$\bullet \qquad \bullet \qquad \bullet \qquad \bullet \qquad \bullet$$

Flaunting the Stars and Stripes and the school flag, Dalton School rises, twelve sheer storeys of greying brick, from the asphalt of East 89th Street. For an hour in the morning and for two-and-a-half hours around noon, a strip of that asphalt — between Park and Lexington Avenues — is closed to traffic so that the children may have a place to play. I thought hard of Rabindra Nath Tagore's words: the image of the Western school is a cage; my school shall be a nest. It is urbanization and industrialization rather than the school itself, that squeeze human beings into Manhattan's every square yard.

Further afield, Dalton rents an outdoor ballfield as well as two gymnasia and a swimming pool. The school's First Program, for children from two to seven, has spread to a specially-designed building on East 91st Street, which has 15 classrooms, a crafts shop, an art studio, a music room, a library, a small tree-shaded play garden in addition to its roof playground.

The main school's twelve storeys house 47 classrooms, including a number specially reserved for laboratory work, a 480-seat theatre and a music theatre; music practice rooms; woodworking, printing and theatrical shops; sculpture, painting and graphics studios; teaching laboratories for the biological and physical sciences; a 30,000-volume library; and a large gymnasium additional to the two that are rented.

The High School, grades nine to twelve, has students from twelve to eighteen years of age. The overlapping of ages is, of course, a reflection of the individualization of each child's study program. A ten-year-old boy or girl may be doing mathematics mainly with the nine-year-olds and English with eleven- or twelve-year-olds. "Children," says Barr, "do not grow up all of a piece."

The basic organizational unit is the individual child. The secondary unit is the "house". In Dalton, a house is a social group of from 16 to 20 children under the guidance of a house advisor.

At age two or three and up to nine, the house is a kind of family group, much like the class of a good infant-school or elementary-school teacher. From Middle School onwards the child is taught by subject specialists. His personal and social development are under the guidance of his house advisor with whom he meets every day. The advisor, says a school brochure, is his "academic counsellor, conscience, and walking report-card".

Is Middle School (from the age of nine or thereabouts) too early for specialized subject teaching? Dalton's answer is, "Not in our conditions". Those conditions include the small groups of 18 or so in place of the average school's forty; a resulting close and secure relationship between child and advisor that is supported by stable tenure of high-quality staff; and encouragement of greater and more successful self-responsibility.

"At every level," Donald Barr insists, "the teacher has to generate the child's critical and self-critical outlook. The teacher has to see each child as a separate educational problem. I hate to hear a teacher say, 'This is a good class. This is a better, or a worse, class than last year's.' Who cares about a class? It is the person who matters."

So when the teacher is checking a child's "contract" — daily in some cases, weekly or monthly as maturity and self-reliance grow — he is not looking for a "pass" mark. The child's responsibility is met by producing the best of which he is capable, not by turning in a "C". It is the teacher's task to know, and to demand, that best. So he may say, "This is good enough for some students, but it isn't good enough for you. You must do it again". Generally, of course, he will also indicate the shortcomings.

At another point, the teacher must anticipate as well as review. To one of two children beginning the same history assignment he will say privately, "This is too easy for you. Leave out that, and that and that . . . and read this and this instead. They are not on the reference list, but you can manage them and you'll find them interesting." To the other child facing exactly the same lithographed assignment sheets he will say, "Don't bother trying to do all of this one. Read this much carefully, and finish the first five questions."

The teacher's perceptiveness is therefore as important as his scholarship. The non-grading of Dalton students is not based on any objective or standardized tests, but on the teacher's intimate knowledge of each child's capacity and potential.

What do the students think of Dalton?

At one level, they are well satisfied. I talked to a small group of nine 13- to 14-year-olds in a Middle School (Grades 7 and 8) psychology class. What would you change in the school if you could have your way? I asked. There were a few blue-skies bids, like turning it into a boarding school and moving it out into the country, with somebody raising the limits and emigrating to Switzerland. More realistically, a pretty, dark-haired girl thought that with 1100 on roll Dalton was now too large: it had lost some of the personal cohesion it had had with 600. She was warmly supported by a blonde classmate. "I'd like to make the classes smaller. When I came here there were only thirteen in a class. Now there are twenty. That's too many. You get cliques who keep apart."

"What about the subjects you study?" I asked.

"Oh, the subjects are fine. What other school lets you do Latin in fifth grade?" (Compulsory Latin kept me out of a university for thirteen years. Fifth-grade Latin was not my personal idea of Paradise, but I understood.)

"And what other school gives you psychology in eighth grade?"

"Or in the seventh?"

"I like the independence here. There's more freedom when you can organize monthly assignments for yourself instead of the teachers telling you what to do every night."

"Ugh, the teachers in my elementary school were terrible. And when you got a bad one you were stuck with her for a whole year."

"I had one for three years. She was awful!"

"I like lab. periods. (Periods for self-chosen study.) I have two labs. a day. You don't get that in other schools."

"Gee, you're lucky, I only have four in a week!"

"Some kids waste their time in labs., though." And the dialogue went off at a tangent. . . .

You can learn a lot about a school just by walking around and looking at its displays and notice boards. In Dalton's ground-floor foyer there is, prominently, a glass case of ceramics created by children from Grades two to eleven; and, as in many schools, the walls are decked with much good and lively child art.

Notice boards advise of current performances of opera and orchestral music; a display at the Whitney Art Museum, a performance by the Dorian Quartet, a season of The Boy Friend; and a clipping from the Lincoln Centre Journal captions a photograph of Dalton School's "Young Children's Orchestra" (first through third grades) with brief details of a forthcoming public performance. From the music theatre adjoining the lobby they, or another group, can be heard in song.

There is a lot of information about overseas study and work programs for the summer vacation period. Jet travel, board, tuition and job placement for a period from six to ten weeks, at prices from $500 to $750 per child, can be organized for England, Switzerland, Italy, Spain, France, Austria, Russia, Scandinavia.

On higher floors the walls bear a display of photography by modern masters of the art; haikus by the poetry class; a direction, by a student group, to those wanting to sign a Peace Pledge to go to the fifth floor, near the elevators; and an announcement "High School Students for McCarthy for President are sponsoring a party at Steve Paul's (301 West 46th St.). Live Band. Free Refreshments. April 30th, 6-9 p.m. $3 donation. $5 a couple."

Barr, one assumes, is neither a Peace Pledger nor a McCarthy supporter. "But," he says, "the school is not out to oppress rational, intellectual criticism of principle. We do not want well-drilled conformists, any more than we want to applaud all rebellion. We want some rebellion and dissent." His compromise with the one-day anti-Vietnam strike of high-school students which happened to take place while I was in New York was to make attendance voluntary for the afternoon of the strike day and to permit an anti-war assembly: a compromise which, admittedly, could be interpreted as Machiavellian in all the circumstances.

Dalton is not without its problems. Indeed, I suspect that its head would claim that its problems are at the heart of its **raison d'etre**. Its fee-paying students must come from the comfortably-off middle classes. Barr is convinced that many children in this social stratum are handicapped by being pampered and mollycoddled. "Some children," he states flatly, "should be kept as far away from their rotten parents as possible. Too many parents are gutless. They are afraid to exercise authority at home because they want to be popular with their children. My school is only a day-school. We exercise authority, not reluctantly, but responsibly, with regard for the individual. If parents abdicate in the home, they are in effect authorizing the child to ignore the school."

So the publishing of notes on "attitudes and behaviour" in the handbook of the Parent-Teacher Association is as much an attempt to educate parents as to advise them of an existing situation. Punctuality, regular attendance, responsibility, integrity are stressed. "Children should practise dignity, style and good manners in school as well as at home." "Children should carry tales neither to each other nor to adults. The habit of gossip is discouraged." (You have to have lived in the sort of Jewish in-group that is a very large part of Dalton's context to appreciate the true flavour of that one.) "Candy and chewing gum are not permitted." "The successful Middle School child does not confuse work and play. . . . He understands that work can be as enjoyable as play. The satisfaction derived from completion of a task is as refreshing as transitory entertainment." And, tartly, last of a dozen injunctions: "Persistent failure to practise constructive attitudes can only lead the School to conclude that it and the child have not achieved a good working relationship."

Not achieving a good working relationship may have a number of aspects. Smoking of "pot" (marijuana) in the school. for example, an increasingly common USA problem, or inducing others to do so, even outside of school hours, brings expulsion from Dalton; not, it is claimed, as punishment but as protection for the school society. A child who smokes outside the school may be allowed to stay on but only on condition that he has therapy. "Pot" is a contentious topic in America as elsewhere, with some authorities claiming it to be less harmful than nicotine or alcohol. Nevertheless, says Barr, Dalton students accept this mandate and do not attempt to argue their "rights" in the matter — though some of the younger members of staff do so on their behalf.

Rebellion against school discipline is treated as a psychological problem and the first and principal effort is to achieve a mutual understanding by patient discussion and guidance. "Formal private schools," says Barr, "can and do expel all the time. They make no concessions. So they have no great problems — on the surface; but pot-smoking, theft and depravity are there all right, under the neat little blazers." Dalton has no school uniform, but insists on the same good taste in dress that teachers exemplify.

Dr. Green, the school psychologist, is the woman who knows many of Dalton's problems close up. Her role varies through advising on admissions, counselling students and teaching of psychology and anthropology.

Admission procedure involves interviews with parents and children and the use of special tests devised to help in deciding whether the child who has been tested, with his physical, emotional, intellectual capacities, is likely to experience real success in the kind of school that Dalton is, with the kind of environment it offers and the demands it makes.

Counselling will often be a matter of taking up with parents the school's or the parents' problems with the child. "I rarely send for a student," says Dr. Greene. "I work with the house advisors. But students come to me, more or less of their own accord."

What sort of problems do the children of the rich and the well-to-do have? Specific difficulties, for example, backwardness in reading, go to the specialists in those areas. Most often the emotional disturbances are home-caused. The small child whose mother has been married three times and who hasn't very definite ideas on who his father is. The girl of 13 who thinks she is adopted but doesn't know for sure. The other 13-year-old who asked Dr. Greene to talk to her mother, now re-married, with a new family of two young children.

"Will you ask her three things: to let me stay up till 9.30 instead of having to go to bed at 8.30; to let me go out on dates just occasionally; and if she can't love me, at least let her act as if she liked me a little."

Mother, duly consulted, was brief and to the point. "I **don't** like her. She reminds me of my ex-husband. I don't like him. I don't like her. Finish!"

"I worked in Harlem for years," says Dr. Greene, "and I didn't ever find that." (And I thought of New York's negro-suburb, Jamaica, Queens, Child-Parent Centre, where every teacher is seen as "a social worker based on the school.")

In Dalton, Dr. Greene has begun a department of behavioural science. In line with Dalton's academic standards, the psychology she takes with the sixteen- and seventeen-year-olds is not merely a study of human relations, but reading and discussion of the original writings of Freud, Adler, Jung and the more modern leaders from Sullavan to Skinner.

The popularity and success of this program led her to introduce anthropology with tenth grade. This led down to a modified psychology-and-anthropology offering for the eleven-to-thirteen age groups with a four-week unit on sex education. In due course, a simpler psychology course will percolate to the fourth-grade level. Later she plans to introduce psychological concepts (not terminology) to the First Program by discussing human behaviour in ways comprehensible at the infants level. Dr. Greene's other part-time vocation is that of psycho-therapist, but she never works with Dalton students in that capacity.

Those unfamiliar with the US pattern should read such a publication as the Dalton PTA Handbook. Apart from school rules and advice running from Dalton Associates and Dalton Traditions through the location of lavatories and pay telephones to details of school programs at different levels of the school, it also lists the five officers and fifty-two parent representatives,* and the fourteen PTA Committees: Art, Bargain Box (fund-raising, thrift-shop pattern), Book and Christmas Fair, Christmas Toy Collection, Community Affairs, Public Education, United Parents, Yorkville Youth Council, Costumes (for Christmas Pageant), International Student Program (hosting), Music, Bookshelf, Saturday Movies, Summer Camp. Many of these are concerned to aid the school, others to give needed voluntary assistance elsewhere in the community.

Parents who are not regular PTA members are kept in touch with the school in a number of ways. They receive school reports, not in the skeletal form of grades and percentages, but as written discussion of their children's development. Twice a year, on "report days", they come to the school specifically to

* Of the whole fifty-seven, one patriarchal male is President

discuss each child with his house advisor. They are urged to read their children's contracts and invited to come — by appointment — to observe classes and laboratory work at any time.

All of this individualized attention costs money, a great deal of money. For 1100 children there is a teaching faculty of 175. Barr suggests that a two-child family needs an income of $25,000 a year to afford Dalton's costs, near $2000 per child per year in higher grades. Even so, the raising of vast sums of additional finance is an eternal preoccupation, since the school aims at a 10% enrolment on scholarships of able but economically poorer children.

Money talks, and what middle-class parental money says is that in the long run it wants its sons and daughters admitted to Harvard, Yale and Vassar. Barr refuses to make or call Dalton a "prep" school cramming adolescents for the examinations instead of educating them according to his lights. So, for senior students, after normal school hours, special examination-preparatory classes are held in which the specific demands of examiners are given more attention. And so, by dint of native ability, a school life of solid academic study, some coaching and, perhaps, the usual modicum of luck, most of the alumni go off to college — a goodly proportion to the most prestigious establishments.

What I think a school like Dalton does is to make you look hard at the total life-pattern of a child before pontificating too readily about what "the" school should do for "the" child. If it is not by any means certain that a rigorous academic diet such as Dalton's is quite the thing for the forty-to-an-undertrained-teacher classes of culturally deprived kids in the slums of the world's great cities, neither is it established that the bright child of indulgent and well-to-do parents in New York's Manhattan will have his life blighted for ever if the school demands intellectual rigour and a stiffening of backbone and sinew.

Almost at the moment of departure I quoted to head master Barr the dictum of George Hilsheimer (of the American Summerhill movement) that, with the declining influence of home and neighbourhood adults, this is the first generation of young Americans that has to grow up without the benefit of a community of human beings on whom to model a life style.

Barr might have said, though he didn't, that this is indeed one of the very needs his teaching staff help to meet. Instead, he bristled a little — he is a vital man who bristles quickly — and responded, "It's also the first generation that has had to grow up without living by its wits, but I see no reason why the human brain should become a vestigial organ on that account."

Granted?

10 Trails out of school

The Pioneer Palace, USSR

In most countries the line between school and non-school activities is the line between compulsion and freedom. In school, however well you are taught, by however well-disposed a teacher, you are there because you must be there — the State, parents, the teachers, singly or in unison have decreed it.

In another too-common model, school is where the child goes in order to learn, and the rest of the day is his "own" time to do as he pleases, to play, to view television, to listen to his own brand of music or read his own kind of books, but not to "learn".

Whatever else is correct, this latter model is wrong. Human creatures are so constructed that they are learning all the time, learning new patterns of thought, feeling and behaviour or learning the re-enforcement of old ones.

The more insightful and intelligent educators become, the more do in-school and out-of-school experiences come to resemble each other. The pre-school child at free play with wisely chosen materials is doing something he wants and needs to do and enjoys doing; but he is also learning his world. The primary school pupil rapt in a piece of creative writing that expresses deep feeling may be at home or in school or in the field, oblivious to which. The secondary school girl who reads the class novel in one night because she is enthralled by it — is she "learning" or "enjoying herself"?

The real line should be drawn between experiences that meet and those that do not meet each dynamic individual's own drive to extend his awareness of the world and his capacity to deal with it: that is, between the experiences that as a freely growing person he wants and those that are forced on him. On this model, there is a strong case for saying that an out-of-school social environment that does not provide the child with widely varying opportunities for constructive growth is as much a restriction as an in-school environment which compels his participation in experiences that fail to match his needs, interests and abilities.

There is something of a contradiction in Soviet education. Schools are pretty formal, rigid, teacher-dominated places where learning is a very serious and exacting business. Yet few societies make freely available to their children the abundant range of opportunities for joyful, active, developmental out-of-school activities that are offered in the Soviet Union. In Moscow alone, 200 trade unions each have a section that arranges games, dances, sports and outings for children. The Union of Writers and Artists and the Actors' Union provide numerous exhibitions and performances especially for children throughout the year. Children's theatre and children's films are substantial, recognized art forms.

And then there are the Pioneer Palaces, one in each of the 18 districts of the city.

The Moscow Palace, known as the "Moscow City Palace of Pioneers and Schoolchildren" is breathtaking by any standards. Palatially designed in great sweeps of stone and glass, its 400 lavish halls and rooms and its spacious sports grounds cover rather more than 90 acres of outer suburban land. The concert hall seats 1000, the theatre 320, the main lecture room 300.

"We try not to duplicate what the schools are doing," said the director. But when I asked him what activities the palace offered, he smiled and shook his head hopelessly and suggested, "Ask me what we don't do. If there is a demand we meet it."

So there are, merely for example, rooms and teachers and equipment for groups whose interests are artistic: drawing, painting, sculpture, poetry, theatre, speech, film, photography, dancing, singing, creative writing. And there are different housekeeping groups, learning about cooking, needlework, interior design and decoration. Children who aren't busy with philately and international friendship by correspondence may join the Young Biologists, or the Young Physiologists or the Young Cosmonauts. That is, if they don't get caught up in the Sports section, the largest of all, which includes swimming, basketball, volleyball, table tennis, skating, gymnastics, acrobatics, football. And competing for attention is the technical department, with radio-electronics, model ships, model aeroplanes, go-karting, television, music recording, radio, Young Drivers . . .

Attendance at the Palace is completely voluntary. "My teachers have to be good," said the director. "If the children don't like them, they simply leave." At one time enrolment was open only to members of the Pioneer organization, a body similar to but more consciously political than the Boy Scouts, which caters for the 9- to 15-year age group. But Moscow City elected to cater for its juniors and its senior students in the one centre, so that any child within the age range is welcome.

The human demand for experience is open-ended, so that the demand for education has no bounds. Only 12,000 children can be admitted to the Moscow City Palace in any one term. They come sometimes in school groups, sometimes in ones and twos, most of them to groups that meet twice a week for an hour and a half to two hours. Ten or fifteen make a group for one activity.

The Palace is open six hours a day on weekdays, with three sessions, the first from 3 p.m. to 5 p.m. (young children finish school at 1.30 p.m.), the second from 5 to 7 and the third 7 to 9. On Saturdays and Sundays the hours are from 10 a.m. to 9 p.m. Tuesday is the weekly holiday. For good measure, some children who attend pre-school in the afternoon shifts come here in the morning; so do convalescing children not yet well enough for normal school classes.

Of the staff of 800, about half are school teachers working at extra (paid) part-time jobs. There is also a core staff whose main employment is at the Palace, though they often hold part-time positions elsewhere. The essential qualifications required are three: you must know your subject; you must be able to teach it; and you must like children. Only compulsory schools, with their traditionally captive audiences, can dispense with that third vital stipulation.

"Everything for the youth, for they are the future," is a Soviet slogan. So the Moscow City Palace is a triumph of modern architecture.

You enter through the Winter Garden, a vast, airconditioned marbled hall, built tall and in contemporary idiom, with paved stone floor and two great, ear-shaped aquaria, one for warm and one for cold-water fish. On the walls, gleaming metal fish swim motionless across decorative metal grilles, and on other grilles hover metal birds, suspended forever in mid-flight. Translucent, reinforced plastic domes in the ceiling admit the sunlight and give extra height for the growing trees. Indoor palms, ferns, plants and flowers in pots are in profusion, and seats for inveterate goldfish-watchers partly surround the pools.

The Winter Garden is a gift, to the Palace and to the children who use it, from the Academy of Sciences. Prominently displayed are a red flag and pictures of Lenin in a gold case, with a large symbolic gold key to the Palace, a gift from the Komsomol (Young Communist) movement to their younger brothers, the Pioneers.

Architecturally, everything is on the grand scale. Nearby the Winter Garden is the largest nursery room you are likely to find anywhere, glasswalled, like an enormous bowl. On low tables stand models of schools and of Pioneer forest camps, small articles of household furniture, toy animals, dolls, blocks, cars, trucks and a particularly large variety of mechanical construction toys and games. To at least some Western eyes (meaning, I suppose, mine) there is something strange in the sight of girls and boys aged up to seven playing with the more childish of these kindergarten toys.

The Young Naturalists have four rooms. Two of these are animal rooms, with the usual marble walls and tiled floors. There is a kind of natural history museum in miniature with very many scores of preserved creatures — fish and octopi and crabs and stuffed birds and a squirrel and a tiger. Then there are numbers of live creatures: in cages, including birds and a monkey, snakes and lizards; a turtle and some fish in small aquaria. Charts line the walls and a gull and a pheasant and other birds wander at large round the floor.

The adjoining plant room is really a greenhouse; and next to it again is a work-and-discussion room with tables and chairs.

The big rooms for model clubs (or groups) have numerous powerful overhead lights, lathes in the wood- and metal-working rooms, and models in various stages of completion. In the parquetry-tiled Exhibition Hall, children's chefs d'oeuvre are displayed in glass cases along with more mature works. And so on, and so on, for 400 rooms, not all of which the less hardy visitor finds the stamina to enter.

Round some of the corridor walls I saw a photographic exhibition, enlargements of work by 15- and 16-year-olds. Sport was the most popular theme, and there were plenty of lively shots of boxing, Rugby, skating, ski-ing, diving, swimming, soccer football. More mature work tended to concentrate on character studies. I can still see one peasant grannie, lifted straight out of Tolstoy, her two teeth like twin milestones in the roadmap network of her wizened face.

I looked in on the theatre, passing on my way to it a rehearsal room where a choir of 30 or so, in Pioneer costume with the striking triangular red neckerchief, were rehearsing their next television performance.

The theatre's drama group has a repertory of six plays, the puppeteers have four. There are two or three early-evening public performances every week, with different children comprising the cast on the different occasions. Audiences, including a few eager parents, come from all over Moscow and fill the theatre. There is no charge for admission, nor is any charge made when professional actors stage children's plays on the same stage.

·   ·   ·   ·   ·

The mood or tone of the Pioneer Palace is probably best compared with that of an adult education class in the West, or, again, that of the Boy Scout movement. What is done is done freely and happily but regarded as important. (Why does one still join those two predicates with "but"?) The teacher does not lecture, he discusses and answers questions. It is taken for granted that those who come, do so in order to learn and to achieve, that they take themselves seriously and ask to be taken seriously in return. So "mucking about" is frowned on, by the group rather than the teacher, or, better, by the group including the teacher, as in a good boys' club. If the activity interests you, let's get on with it. If it doesn't, nobody is forcing you, go join another group, or do something in one of the special individual work rooms; or just go home.

The aim of Pioneer Palace activity is general rather than specific. Somewhere in the background is a theory that is expressed negatively as "Satan finds some mischief still for idle hands to do", or, more positively, in the faith of Homer Lane that "every destructive act is due to a constructive instinct that has been denied its proper expression". The education gained at the Moscow Pioneer Palace is seen as valuable in itself, fully justifying the cost, 1.5 million roubles a year. If the student gains a worthwhile hobby, that is sufficient. If he shows outstanding ability, then the Soviet has a masterly art of mopping up every dram of human talent, and the hobby may turn into a vocation.

You don't have to be a Communist to want Pioneer Palaces for your children. I was impressed, as much as anything, by the notion of sharing (of which Communism has no monopoly) built into the work of the Moscow City Palace of Pioneers and School Children. If you learn, there is a moral obligation to teach. And a large honour board was covered with hundreds of certificates stating that "Svetlana M. learned Armenian, Cossack and Georgian folk dances and taught them to a group at her school"; and that "Vladimir P. studied model aeroplane construction and led a group in Grade 9".

Life is dynamic equilibrium, and if anything was perfect it would no longer be dynamic. I like to think of children having plenty of time to discover and explore, to fantasy and invent, away from even the kindliest adult guidance. Still, if any government wants to build Pioneer Palaces or their equivalent round my neighbourhood, then on behalf of my children, I'll take the risk. I'll even pay my share of the tax.

11 When is a school?

Youth Town and School. Denmark

In the city of Copenhagen, the suburb of Rodovre contains a town: Youth Town. And Youth Town contains a school. And the whole "experimental centre" as it is called arose from an idea of Borge Lorentzen.

Mr. Lorentzen, a successful and well-to-do architect, has two enthusiasms, building and youth. On a piece of sound but marshy land in Rodovre, some 1.7 acres in extent, he set a number of building apprentices to work, using machines and tools lent by a world-famous petroleum company, to drain the marsh and begin erecting buildings as "masterpieces".

Now Denmark is a small affluent country that has not yet completely replaced the personal ethos of community living by the impersonal mass culture of Super-city. There is a strong tradition of public-spiritedness in Copenhagen, where the overseas tourist goes for a free tour and refreshment at the Carlsberg brewery, sixth largest in the world, which was presented to the community by its founders, to go on perpetually earning profits for the support of science, art and education.

Consequently, it was well within the Danish tradition that the petroleum company offered to sponsor a go-karting centre — a sort of service workshop — as part of the building operations in the newly-developing area. Then the same company added the idea of a kind of home science centre where girls and boys might learn about the domestic use of oil and the non-domestic use of cosmetics (which are made from petroleum).

Prompted by Mr. Lorentzen, other firms began to see advantages in this type of public relations exercise that combined philanthropy and advertising. Gradually there developed a kind of consortium that included the Ministry of Education and representatives of trades, industries and workers, to plan and erect an innovative Centre including the Youth Town.

The site, now expanded to eleven acres, includes a government-built junior high school; the petroleum building (not, as it transpired, for go-karting); insurance buildings and a bank donated by the appropriate commercial groups; a small supermarket, the only project on which three fiercely competitive firms collaborate; and a town hall, given by Danish labour organizations, a post-office, and a building for "family education" given by the savings banks.

Danish employer organizations added a counselling centre to which young people may go for expert advice on the choice of a vocation. Since this gift might smack too much of self-interest, for good measure they threw in half-a-million kronor (about $100,000 U.S.) for a 300-seat theatre which is yet (1968) to be built with the aid of the apprentice craftsmen.

The church building for Youth Town was financed by 4-cent donations from a million Danish schoolchildren, designed (free of charge) by another prominent architect and built, as far as possible, by a team of fifteen carefully-chosen apprentices, using materials of which many were donated by their manufacturers.

The whole concept is not so much one of a school plus a town, but rather of a town that includes a school. So the other buildings planned and under construction on the site include classroom blocks; halls of residence for pupils from outside Copenhagen and for teachers attending training courses; a cafeteria; units equipped for practical training in wood and metal work, engine repairs, building and construction work; a laboratory for agriculture and gardening; a hall of instruction; a hall for cultural functions; and so on. Since the students' learning experiences take them into all the buildings on the site for varying periods, it is a pretty puzzle in semantics to decide where the Rodovre "school" begins and ends.

The pupils of Rodovre school are not specially selected for attendance. They are the neighbourhood boys and girls of grades 8, 9 and 10, aged, that is, from 13-plus to 16-plus.

The school is an experimental one, devoted to the working out of new educational curricula and methods. It is planned on the usual spacious Scandinavian lines. The metal workshop is as large as a comfortable three-bedroomed house (over 1000 square feet), the engineering workshop three-quarters of this size, and the wood-working plus fitting and turning area is as big as the others put together. Classrooms for 24 students contain 560 square feet, an area in which most countries still herd 40 children.

(I asked the principal whether groups were generally larger than 24. He became apologetic about huge classes in some schools. "You see," he said, "there is a teacher shortage", and then went on to explain that, as Danish people became more affluent, they found 24's and 30's intolerable in beginner classes and began sending their children to private schools where there could be classes of ten or fifteen for more personal attention.)

"Bridge-building" was a phrase I heard often in Rodovre. Students learning commerce and domestic science and civics not only find themselves at work in the bank or the insurance company or the shopping area or the town hall. They also have talks and discussions, in and out of classroom situations, with workers from the same places; and their syllabuses are frequently planned by teachers and representatives of trade, commerce and industry.

Similar "bridge-building" links agriculture and the workshop skills to the ongoing business of the adult world.

From their side, the banks and life assurance companies and the post office are not engaged in a one-way traffic. Their bridge-building, they insist, is a matter of trying out and perfecting new ideas in Rodovre and then using them in the wider community.

On another level again, there is much co-operation amongst teachers, students and parents, with regular "information meetings" attracting almost 100% of parents and with parents frequently visiting the school during working hours. Interestingly, a standing invitation to contact the teachers for personal discussions is almost never availed of. The principal wondered whether this reluctance reflected the reticence of Western society's early adolescents to appear conspicuous.

Rodovre's version of general studies (the bridge to the larger world) is translated into English as Orientation. This is something of a catch-all subject, combining elements of geography, history, literature, and what the Danes call biology but we should describe as sociology.

Current events provide the starting point for much of the work in Orientation — racism, war, new scientific developments. In other subjects of the Danish high school curriculum, the teacher's professional freedom extends only to methods of teaching, but in Orientation he chooses both method and content. Here in Rodovre a pattern of content and method may lead from a broad current-events-social-studies approach to a deeper study of psychology and of one foreign culture (China or South Africa, for example) and thence to a thorough exploration of the literature of one non-Danish language (in translation, necessarily). Film, music and art are involved in cultural studies — jazz as an aspect of the American negro's culture (or sub-culture), for example, or Bergman film as one reflection of Swedish life. Much of the work is by individual and group assignment and report, on topics self-chosen from a very extensive list.

Eventually, too, this kind of school work leads out (bridge-builds) to its counterpart in real life. In company with the form teacher each class makes a carefully prepared two-weeks visit to a country town of Denmark, investigating the way of life of the community and reporting back to school and parents in speech, film, art and writing. Beyond this again are international tours. The Class 10 to whom I spoke were busy planning a twelve-day visit to Yugoslavia.

Thus Rodovre Experimental Centre from the viewpoint of its permanent students, looking out to the wider world. There is, however, a reverse flow, into the centre.

As of 1971 large numbers of 9th and 10th grade country children (between 3000 and 4000) are to be brought in for 14-day residential courses throughout the school year. During their stay they are given an opportunity to gain a working familiarity with a chosen two out of a fifteen-subject range that makes use of the Youth Town facilities — agriculture, commerce, clerical work, domestic work and so on, alphabetically, to social work and woodwork. During the same period the teachers of each group consult with Rodovre staff who have the duty of developing new curricula and methods.

One question troubling the mind of an educator was whether the total impact of all this structuring of school into affluent society and vice versa might be to create a cosy sense of warmth and security inside an isolated enclave. I was assured that this danger had been considered and that at least part of the counter-measure lay in Orientation, taught as a humane study, given the largest time-table allotment of all the subjects, and generating active work for UNICEF and other international organizations. Perhaps. . . . And in the end we shall never quite know how strong was one social-educational influence amongst many.

Meanwhile Mr. Lorentzen is off to other parts of Copen-hagen, pioneering a series of adventure playgrounds that include provision for apprentices to put up buildings in them.

It's the sort of thing they do well in Denmark.

12 Scholar-ships

School at Sea. England

Two of Britain's smallest-sized boarding schools have the largest enrolments, having helped to educate a quarter of a million boys and girls in the last seven years. These are the school ships of British India, currently the S.S. "Nevasa" and the S.S. "Uganda", and the two title words, "school" and "ship", are of equal importance.

Actually, to make up the quarter-million you have to count the passengers of "Dunera" and "Devonia", converted troopships which were replaced by the "Uganda" as recently as 1968. "Nevasa", larger of the two present vessels, is of 21,000 tons. She can carry 1100 pupils in dormitories and an additional 307 cabin passengers. The smaller school, "Uganda", 17,000 tons, accommodates 920 pupils and 305 cabin passengers.

Both ships spend all their days, from year's end to year's end, plying from Southampton, Leith, Greenwich, Swansea, Liverpool and London's Tilbury docks to foreign parts, normally those of northern Europe in the summer months and southern Europe in autumn, winter and spring.

Educational cruises last for between two and three weeks. Often they are "block booked" by a British local education authority for children of schools within its area. On other occasions, groups from different parts of Great Britain make up the passenger list. Overseas visitors to the U.K. join the tours. On one tour the "Uganda" became an international school, carrying some 400 children from Cornwall and Devon, a few score more from other areas of England, 100 French children, and 60 Japanese fitting the cruise into a longer tour.

Let me talk about S.S. "Uganda" which I know at first hand.

From the viewpoint of the student, preparations for an edu-

93

cational cruise on the ship at sea may commence, as much as eighteen months before sailing date, with the problem of finding the fare. The amount involved is somewhere within £10 sterling ($24 U.S.) of £40 ($96 U.S.), plus pocket money up to £10. For some children it is no problem. For others, and those usually the ones who stand to gain most from the stimulus of travel, the amount looms so large that the education authorities subsidize their trips. My elementary mathematics turns up the interesting finding that to afford every child in the nation one such tour between the ages of ten and sixteen would add an extra £7 per pupil per year to the cost of education.

In the months immediately preceding a tour, teachers direct some of the school work towards the forthcoming journey. Over the years, techniques for doing this have been thoughtfully and thoroughly developed.

Thus, I have on my desk a typical preparatory booklet of sixty large pages, well but not expensively reproduced by photo-lithographic process. Titled "Northern Cruise" it bears on its cover a bust of a fearsome Viking, sword and shield in hand, the prow of his longship visible in the background.

Within, the different segments of the book are of differently coloured paper. **"Birmingham Junior Schools Cruise, 'Uganda', from Friday, 17th May to Monday, 27th May, 1968"**, says the title page. Then follows a table of contents — General Information, Useful Information, Ships and the Sea, the Journey, Maps Section.

Throughout, an attempt is made to link study and journey realistically to the interests of the 900 ten-to-twelve-year-olds from 40 junior schools. Since the itinerary leads from Tilbury to the Kiel Canal, thence to Copenhagen, Eidfjord and Bergen, there are maps of the journey, and brief verbal sketches accompanied by line drawings of each of the ports of call. History notes and sketches take the Viking theme further. Useful phrases in Danish and Norwegian, such as "Thank you", "How much?" words for numbers one to ten, provide interesting introductory instances of comparative language. The mathematics teacher introduces the 24-hour clock and the business of exchanging foreign currency. And throughout, there is information about ships and the sea in general and this ship in particular, and nautical terms and sleeve markings, and deck games, and flags of the nations and so on — purposive reading and comprehension.

For juniors, the touch is light, the content limited. For senior groups, longer and more detailed study precedes the journey. The City of Aberdeen's preparatory booklet was magnificent and lavishly illustrated in four colours with much more detailed treatment.

"Uganda" is fairly tightly structured as both school and ship. Two factors are paramount, space and safety. A very large assembly hall holding just under 400 is used for regular lectures and films. A number of classrooms, each with room for from 20 to 30 students, open off the deck; they are complete classrooms, with desks and blackboards; and a good deal of time is given over to normal lessons. There is a small reference library. There is also recreation space, inevitably limited. And the potential of 1000 children, if they are let loose, for activities that might be harmless enough on land but dangerous or tragic afloat means that rules about who is to be where and when are strictly enforced.

The teaching staff, or, more broadly, the adult educating group on board, is in three main categories. The ship's director of education and his assistant are professional, graduate teachers with wide experience of the sea and the countries visited. Two senior students from a college of Physical Education sail on each voyage, their P.E. work en route being regarded as a valuable part of their training.

In another category, with every 15 students comes at least one teacher. Finally, some of the cabin passengers, whose area of the ship is semi-detached from the children's, are often willing and able to put knowledge and talents at the disposal of the learners.

Apart from teaching staff, the "Uganda" has the normal complement of officers and crew, including six matrons, two nurses and two doctors. There is a hospital equipped for all but major operations: on occasion an appendix has been removed there.

Entertainment is scheduled. The principle, learned and developed the hard way over years of experience, is to keep the children occupied all the time. From reveille at 7.00 a.m. to lights out at 9.30 p.m. (or 10 p.m for seniors) there is a program that allows free time — in specified areas of the ship — but offers many lectures, films, lessons, games and the usual shipboard events. Inevitably, some students feel some of the restrictions to be unfortunate, as, indeed, within limitations of space, they must be; but in general, most find the routine tolerable and many — for better or for worse — prefer their time to be fully organized.

By British standards, there is compensation for all of this. Partly because it has been, traditionally, so much of a privilege of the upper classes, the British attach very great importance to the experience of boarding school. British India officials in charge of the school ships, both the people in head office in London and those on the "Uganda", were insistent that this was a basic value of any educational tour. "If the ship never left the quay," they said, "the experience would still be worth while." Inspectors of the Department of Education who accompanied one tour endorsed this opinion. For many of the boys and girls involved this was the first experience of leaving the security of home and family, of accepting a measure of responsibility for household/shipboard chores (tidying, bunk-making and the rest), of learning to live from day to day with other people of their own ages but different backgrounds, country child with city child, Londoner with Glaswegian, government school student with pay school student. Again, in closer proximity, teachers and pupils see in each other dimensions not apparent in every school's normal environment.

Characters develop. The mouse-like adolescent girl who is, at home and school, the model of a demure ear'y Victorian daughter and pupil, may become the life and soul and chief organizer of the concert party. So I was repeatedly assured. No doubt, shipboard being shipboard, other forms of maturation ensue. But dormitories are segregated and guarded, and the ship is assiduously patrolled twenty-four hours a day.

Different cruise schedules can be worked out for each tour in conjunction with the schools. Spain and the Mediterranean countries are immensely popular, because of numerous historical and cultural links to Britain. Some tours venture to Turkey and Egypt, when the political climate is propitious. Genoa, Piraeus, Malta. Lisbon, Beirut, Haifa. Trondheim, Oslo, Amsterdam. Thirty years ago H. G. Wells, more forward-looking than most, wrote of ageing adult tourists of his day doing at fifty the travelling that might have educated them at twenty. British children are beginning at ten.

One ambitious tour took a group of sixth-form students and a team of university lecturers on a three-weeks' tour to West Africa. History, geography, economics, politics, psychology, anthropology, sociology, marine biology and astronomy were tailored to the ship's progress, and student and teacher switched from tutorial to dancing and from dancing to tutorial as occasion arose. Three weeks, however, seemed to be long enough, even for sixth formers. When longer distances are involved, the company now flies students on either forward or return leg of the journey.

What does an educational cruise give? I selected parts of a few reports from a host of news sheets and magazines with names like *Wavelength* and *Viking Verity* and *Cruisader*. Some of these publications were prepared on board, others were written back at school. The first poem, "The Cruise", is by a 12-year-old boy from a secondary modern school.

> "The Cruise
> My first impressions of the ship were
> Sleeping under the water line on a top bunk,
> Being away from home,
> Sleeping with my school mates,
> Being abroad for the first time,
> Seeing cheap things sold dear.

Sailing for days on end,
Seeing nothing but the sea,
Eating whilst in motion
From a tray instead of a plate.
The smells of the Kasbah,
Seeing cars different from the English
Driving on the right,
Seeing palm trees on the streets
And money problems all the time.
Unfamiliar clothes on strange people,
Seeing poor houses in narrow streets,
Women's faces veiled,
Carrying heavy blankets on their heads
And small babies on their backs,
Hearing weird music and hoarse voices
Forever persuading us to buy
Their wares.
And remembering all the while,
That we were far away from home."

"Lisbon was our next destination. We passed the Tower of Belem and Prince Henry the Navigator's monument. We enjoyed our day in Lisbon more than I can say. I shall never forget the wonderful buildings and squares. The pavements were mosaic and the patterns delightful to look at. We were delighted to see the fish and fruit sellers carrying their wares in baskets on their heads, and the knife grinder who sat on the side of the road, sharpening knives and scissors. The shops were magnificent and I bought some wonderful gifts to take home to my family.

The days passed all too quickly. We swam in the ship's pool and played deck games of all kinds. Our lessons went on. We wrote essays, drew and coloured maps and collected pictures for our school and our individual scrap books. We prepared for the ship's concert, but the days were all too short.

To our great joy we found that we had won four prizes. We sailed past the Channel Islands; we were nearing France and Cherbourg, our last port of call before Southampton."

"I remember visiting Stockholm on one cruise and in the harbour we passed an outward bound freighter laden with coniferous timber — pit props at a guess. Here was an excellent starting point for a discussion in one of the ship's classrooms later in the voyage. I always encourage boys to look at other ships in the harbours we visit and to note imports and exports. The unloading of British products in foreign ports, invariably motor cars, is always interesting. Observation is the keynote and there is so much to see. Sometimes it is possible to penetrate the country further and to travel away from the port. One such example is Malaga in Southern Spain. Malaga, a town of 30,000

people has an interesting castle and a beach and provides the
boys with a fair picture of life in that part of Spain. When time
permits, the boys can go, at extra cost, on a twelve-hour coach
excursion to Granada. The main reason for going is to see the
beautiful palace of the Alhambra but the seventy miles of extra-
ordinary countryside provide an excellent practical geography
lesson. In Malaga the trees are laden with oranges by the side of
the road. As the road climbs, the vegetation changes and citrus
gives way to cork, vines, olives and sisal. Sometimes the coaches
stop to allow the boys to cut a specimen of cork bark for themselves. The land is barren and wooden ploughs drawn by oxen can
be seen frequently. Malaga is not an isolated example. At Haifa,
too, the boys were invited to pick an orange for themselves from
the lush orange groves along the side of the road to Jerusalem.
A very different type of farming can be seen when the boys are
taken by coach from the docks at Copenhagen to the castle at
Elsinore. Here intensive Danish dairy farming can be seen. . . .

"We land at Oslo.
       Why does the land go up and down and up and down?
It doesn't normally. At least I can't remember it being so
shaky before. I suppose that I am just suffering from land
sickness. Anchors aweigh!
We saw round Oslo.
       The King quickly left once he saw us!
We arrive at Leningrad.
       'Welcome to our citee.'
       'You are our friends.'
       'Peace and Friendship.'
       What a welcome. They even brought the town band.
And it's the first time we've been given flowers.
We go sightseeing in Leningrad.
       They have rain here too!
       We buy postcards, we buy dolls.
We visit Helsinki.
       Lovely modern architecture. Lovely HIGH prices. We
didn't get a sauna bath.
Copenhagen.
       First letter home. The stamps are cheap here.
       We have a glorious shopping spree in this fairytale
city. We think the Danes are great!
We return home.
       We were rushing while we were ashore. Now we are
rushing on board ship. Did we catch something in Leningrad?"

Experiences of the world come in two categories, mediated
and immediate. Spellbound by the delights of modern technology,
we are sometimes apt to forget that the vicarious experience it

offers is still vicarious. However artistically designed and presented, the all-sound, technicolour, music-backed or television travelogue is still somebody else's direction to observe this, to hear that, to treat one matter as important, another as trivial, and others — edited or unnoticed by the film-maker — as non-existent. In compensation, of course, we see and hear many things that we would otherwise miss on a personal odyssey, for lack of time or opportunity or the unseasonableness of our visit: Fujiyama's cone is visible on only 80 days in a year, for instance, and you need a full moon to see the Taj Mahal at its best, and every country has its Spring and New Year Festivals.

So there is a place — and an important place — for learning the world, not only by word of book but by recorded sight and sound. But this being said, there is also a need, which technology and economics and ingenuity are beginning to meet, for first-hand experience of distant places, and first-hand meetings with people of other cultures in their own environments. Here the traveller does not merely see and hear, but see, hear, smell, touch, taste and sense, in ways that no mechanical device can imitate. More than this, he becomes his own master, his own educator, as he brings to the total experience the ever incomplete totality that is himself, to see and hear and feel and all the rest, in his own unique way that is never quite the same as anyone else's, to make his own unique re-structuring of the big, blooming, buzzing multi-sensory kaleidoscope; so that he himself is individually enriched and the world is thereby enriched also, as the richer person bears within him new thoughts and feelings that are the potential for poem or story or picture or song or talk that will be his contribution to the enrichment of others.

A thousand years of history as an island nation testify to Britain's strategically favourable situation for taking advantage of the school ship concept as an educational development. Yet already the aeroplane can compete with the ship in economy of travel, and university students from Australia fly thousands of miles to every country on earth to live the lives of other peoples during the long vacation.

Australia is an affluent country, but others are equally so, and few have so great a barrier of distance to overcome. The principle comes first, then the adaption to local conditions. If travel can be an integral part of what we really mean by education, then British India's "Nevasa" and "Uganda" and Australia's aeroplanes are trail-breakers to new and exciting possibilities for young people everywhere.

13 You've got to care

Senior High School. USA

De Witt Clinton High School in New York's Bronx has eight counsellors in its College Advisory Office. But THE Clinton counsellor, by right of seniority, common consent and personal charisma is 55-ish dynamic, wisecracking, cigar-smoking Dr. Seymour Bernhard.

Dr. Bernhard is a businessman. He buys boys on the open market, processes them through De Witt Clinton, and disposes of them to U.S. colleges and universities at considerable profit — to themselves, and the institutions, and the prestige of De Witt Clinton.

This is only one part of the picture. Unmodified, it is unfair, not only to the school and its principal, Walter J. Degnan, but also to Dr. Bernhard. And yet it is a good enough first model of the mainspring by which Clinton ticks.

I lecture in the field of philosophy of education. Regularly on Mondays and Wednesdays, between 10.00 a.m. and 10.55 I explain, in carefully-chosen academic syllables, precisely what is wrong with education and the state of the nation and Western culture and human civilization and the planet and the universe in general. I do so with my hand on my heart, knowing right deep down to my innermost bone marrow that if only the human race would shift the world and the universe and civilization and Western culture and the Australian nation in the direction in which my other hand so unerringly points, then the basic problems of education and life would be solved. (For the remaining details, check my lectures in educational methodology, Tuesdays and Thursdays, from 3 to 4 p.m.)

At the time of writing (October, 1968) the human race is still proving astonishingly obdurate. A great deal of this book is devoted to the work of people who, until the process of racial enlightenment is completed, have re-moulded their corner of the educational globe nearer to heart's and mind's desire. And this is excellent and as it should be.

But on other fronts, dedicated and able people labour not with what might be, but with — and all too frequently against — what is. On Monday mornings, when the hands of the clock point to 9 a.m., and a hundred and a thousand and a million students, willing and unwilling, bright and slow-developing, co-operative and obstreperous, products of our present uncelestial world troop into the schools, then lessons must begin. Imperfect teachers with imperfect students in imperfect conditions must get on with the job; and in the classrooms, at that moment, the most eloquent and inspired lectures on Plato and Dewey and Martin Buber are of limited relevance.

This is the portrait of a school, working under the quite intolerable pressures of the here and now that afflict so many of the developing and developed countries. De Witt Clinton should not have 6000 senior high school students and only 4500 seats for them to sit on, as any even reasonably adequate educational theoretician can prove: but it does have them. Nor should it have senior high boys aged 16 reading and calculating at the third grade level: but they are there. In any well-run republic, there really ought not to be so many adolescents so hardened against education that 1200 to 1500 absences on a single day are not unusual and 250 of last year's theoretical intake never showed up at all: but that is the situation. If the unlovelier crannies of the Bronx have spawned school-age junkies on hundred-dollar-a-day narcotics diets — lads who will strip cars of tyres and wheels and pillage homes of radios and television to get dollars for the drugs their inner demons crave — why, this is a Bad Thing and a very black mark against slum conditions: but there they are, these young-old toughs, right on campus, sitting — irregularly — in the algebra class and the English tutorial awaiting the teachers' pedagogic ministrations.

And yet, in high-ranking McCall's Magazine, February 1968, two high-ranking educationists, Grace and Fred M. Hechinger, listed an even dozen of public high schools in New York where it is still possible to get a good education; and De Witt Clinton is one of the twelve.

Is it entirely obvious that attaining this kind of reputation, in this sort of conditions, is any less an achievement than creating a splendid up-to-date school with hand-picked well-to-do children at a thousand dollars a semester?

Perhaps not entirely.

"Job hunting?" asks the New York subway car's hoarding. "Take a look at your opposition." And the rest of the advertisement features a quartet of smiling graduates, capped and gowned. The match-flap is more peremptory in style. "Drop-outs, stay in school", it commands. And the cover of a little four-page pamphlet advises, "A college education is worth $100,000 in a working lifetime."

In the USA, higher education is a competitive climb to status and the hope of economic security. But how do you ease the grade for the less capable and the almost capable and the given-up-for-lost, in a school so short of places that it works overlapping shifts?

"We do what we can," says Principal Degnan. And the first thing is to decide what can be achieved, and to plan for it with the efficiency that characterizes any other large-scale organization with similar problems. So the hopeless cases — those who not only cannot but will not participate and who are merely the prisoners of well-intentioned leaving-age regulations — these are given a very low priority. You can get a good education at Clinton, but there is one proviso: you have to want it, or at least be open to being persuaded to want it.

"I'm a businessman," says Seymour Bernhard, "and I like to win." (He runs his own highly successful international travel business on the side.) "Winning" in this context means getting boys into Clinton, organizing both their education and a liaison network into the tertiary education institutions of the nation, and getting the right boy into the right college where he can succeed.

Organization really goes back to 1951 when De Witt Clinton, once the largest school in the world, had shrunk to a beggarly 2200 and was still shrinking. Academically it was far from good: no successes in one year's State Regents' Scholarship Examinations and only one in another year. The newcoming rival, Bronx High School of Science, five minutes' walk away, was threatening to drain off the most able. Clinton seemed fated to become a vocational school relegated to the minor league.

"The job," said Bernhard, "was to develop a package that could be sold to kids and their parents: first-rate teachers; sound academic tuition in mathematics, physics, languages; sport; and, above all else, care for the individual.

"Over the years," he recalls, "I had to sell the idea that colleges are interested in the student's ranking in his high school, as well as in his percentage mark. A boy with 92%* here will be in the top 4% of Clinton; but he will be only at the top of the bottom third in the Bronx High School of Science."

So the package was made and the selling campaign succeeded.

---

* It is instructive to the foreign visitor like myself to note how often examination percentages are bandied as if they were an unassailable hallmark of quality.

In the early fifties, Clinton was 80% white. In 1963 it was still 72% white. Today, in 1968, as the city's socio-economic groups are polarized and the middle-class whites phototropically seek their kind in the outer areas the percentage of whites is nearer 40, with approximately another 40% negro and the remaining 20% Puerto Rican.

Unlike BHSS, Clinton must take all comers. Yet it still sees itself, aggressively, as a college preparatory high school as well as an all-abilities school, a cosmopolitan school where, though many students are living on relief, there are still boys whose fathers earn $50,000 dollars a year — twice the salary of the school principal and $4000 a year more than the chief-school-custodian-engineer. Clinton aims to be a democracy of income as well as of ability.

"You've got to **care**!" says Dr. Bernhard. "Care to win and care for boys." In that order? Chronologically at least, it comes the other way about, and much of the caring is done in the first years, by principal and staff and departmental chairmen. College guidance comes into its own later.

The records of each of the nearly two thousand applicants every year are scrutinized by the chairmen of the school's eleven departments. From the first profile of a boy's performances, his strengths, weaknesses and special talents, each chairman will make a tentative decision as to how many courses the student should attempt in his particular department.

On paper, the system of study credits is similar to that (described earlier in this book) for Bronx High School of Science, except that Clinton offers both an academic diploma and a general or non-academic one, and allows a wider freedom for choice — in consultation. Rather more than half of the 34 credits needed for an academic diploma are laid down as either required minor studies (art, health, music) or required majors (English, social studies, economics, World History and American History). Four units of science and two each of algebra and geometry are also required, and must be incorporated in the choices made amongst elective majors: so that, ultimately, some sciences and some mathematics become major studies. For the general diploma, 32 units are required, and the provisions regarding choice of content of courses are relaxed a little.

One of the advantages of the very large school is that it can afford to offer a wide range of options and levels, both within and across subjects. "If we want thirty-five left-handed piccolo players," I was told, "we just hustle around and find them." More relevant, you can also find thirty-five students at an advanced level to make up a class in philosophy. If a hundred want to study computer technology, you can buy a $25,000 machine. Suppose you had seven? So Clinton can have thirty-six types of English classes, from advanced placement and honours standard literature

for the college-bound, to remedial reading and speech therapy*
at the lower end of the range, with special classes in journalism,
dramatics, creative writing and public speaking.

Once the student is started on his course, various organizational devices are at work to guide and assist him. If his all-
important percentages fall below the minimum necessary for him
to achieve his diploma, departmental chairmen and teachers are
at work, figuring possible remedial measures or changes in
courses. Report cards go home to parents, sometimes with help-
ful effect, though all too often the home situation is impossible.
("Many of the kids have no home. It's only a deposit box. Their
real home is **here**," says Dr. Bernhard, who cares.) If a parent
disagrees with a boy's placement (in academic or general stream,
for example) he is invited to discuss the situation with the departmental chairman. If a scholarship-seeking boy wants special
assistance, he gets it. If a boy who is dropping behind needs extra
summer school work in the long vacation to try to pick up the
necessary units, it is available to him. There is a proviso, of
course, one already mentioned: the student has to be around the
school — he has to want an education. (What do three truant
officers do on Tuesday morning when 1500 students are absent?)

At one end of the problem spectrum are boys with IQ's of
up to 125, who should be achieving honours but who are actually
failing subjects. A woman teacher† is a co-ordinator of studies
for between two hundred and three hundred under-achievers,
checking their backgrounds, keeping in touch with parents, arranging more special programs.

For the boys who become identifiable as potential drop-
outs, various work-oriented programs are developed. Some of
these are "sandwich" courses of familiar patterns. They range
from those where the student works for half a day in industry and
half in school, to others where the work and study halves of the
sandwich are digested in six-monthly slices.

Two carefully selected sixty-strong groups of students not
following the academic program take special courses leading towards employment as firemen and policemen. Officers of the
police or fire departments co-operate in leading the courses.

At the time of my visit Clinton was still feeling rather good
about its relatively new study program for aspiring zoo-keepers,
the only such program in the country. School "stock" included
monkeys, raccoons, birds of various breeds, boa constrictors,
alligators, sloths and ant-eaters.

---

* Separate units and half units are: Speech Correction, Foreign Accent,
Speech Clinic (for stutterers).

† Although Clinton's students are all male, the staff are male and female,
about 50-50.

Zoo-keeping is the sort of study course about which progressive and traditional educators argue interminably. Is is education or merely training? The boys' sandwich course included English, mathematics and social studies, modified (it is a kindly term) to their non-academic ability level. A biology teacher, in consultation with zoo authorities, had developed appropriate study units. Ecology and animal psychology (not merely animal behaviour, I was assured) were involved, realistically enough. No doubt the English teacher read with more than normal gusto Whitman's "I think I could turn and live with animals" to boys who were doing just that for a significant part of their time — gaining, they told me, a much more intimate knowledge of their charges than is possible among the far larger animal populations of a city zoo.

What makes a school? In Manhattan's 1968 four-column telephone directory, pages 1681 to 1706 are devoted to listing institutions that claim the title on the grounds that in them somebody teaches something to somebody else. There are schools for art and auto mechanics, business and beauty, cards and comptometry, dramatics and dog grooming, and so on to the (Jewish) Yeshiva schools and the yoga schools, passing hypnosis and insurance selling (which are separate courses) and judo, karate and linoleum laying along the alphabetical way.

All of these schools are primarily business concerns which seek paying students. By arrangement, some of the boys for whom, after fair trial, formal English and eighteenth-century history have come to seem too far from the real world to induce enthusiasm for study receive a week's free tuition from a number of the more reputable job-oriented schools. A boy who finds that a study program in barbering or the printing trade or air conditioning makes more sense to him will try to gain entry to a vocational school offering such a course. Should he succeed, that is that, Should he fail, however, he will discuss with a guidance officer the possibility of paying fees to the private business in order to acquire skill and training in some area where he can reasonably hope that the machine is not going to replace him in the next decade.

Clinton's principal, Walter Degnan, could fairly claim that, if any boy, average or far below average, has some ability and desire to learn, the school is doing its best to help him.

But at the other end of the spectrum, Clinton's public image, in an image-worshipping age and culture, is closely linked to its students' performances in gaining scholarships and colleges places.

Dr. Bernhard's official title is Co-ordinator of the College Advisory Office. His eight-man team is the largest of its kind in New York, separate from though closely allied to the ten-man guidance and counselling team for earlier years.

The College Advisory Office is really the focal point for two great, fan-shaped communications networks. The internal one catches up every college-place-seeking boy in the school and files him away in two entries: here at the hub in the filing cabinets as a card-indexed performance and personality profile; and in the minds of the advisors as a human being with goals and abilities, strengths, weaknesses, a history and needs and desires. The external grapevine covers every tertiary institution in the USA, its offerings and requirements.

"Now take any card here," said Dr. Bernhard, pulling open a long drawer and selecting a card at random. "Oh, yes — Paul J. His average is 82 or better each year. He'll get a place easily enough. Paul could get into Z College here in New York and he has enough ability to graduate there; but the trouble is they make their first-year courses very demanding and Paul is always inclined to feel crushed if he isn't succeeding straight away. It would be much better for Paul to go to Q. in Illinois. It's a nice, comfortable place where they look after their freshmen very well, and it will get him away from that military old father of his who's the cause of most of his uncertainty in the first place."

I would make a small wager that Paul ends up as a graduate of Q.

De Witt Clinton is the only high school where a student may not apply to a university or college without first obtaining the school's permission. The logic is impeccable. This is not Bronx High School of Science where everybody is top-line and everybody is going to college and everybody at or near the top knows he's going to be welcomed by the most prestigious institutions. This is Clinton where you've had to work damned hard to reach reasonable college level, and if fifteen of you at just about that level all apply to a college which traditionally takes only five or six Clinton boys, then the rest are going to be rejected. Let's spread the talent and find places for the whole lot. Now, there's a lovely college in New Jersey, not very big, but it offers . . .

So Dr. Bernhard runs his fingers through the file cards of past and present students and his mental fingers through the index of memory. "In some out-of-state schools, a New York education is a disadvantage. A Clinton lad can easily become the butt of the locals, especially if he's been overprotected. Like David C. here, who's going to X. So of course I wrote ahead to another Jewish Clinton boy who's been in X for two years, to contact David as soon as he arrives and look after him for a while.

"And here's Jackson R. They want 80% in J. College, and Jackson's only a 78% boy. But he's a good lad and he comes from a terribly disadvantaged home and he'll do better, so I wrote to them, and they're taking him in.

"And here's Donald M., a negro lad. He was found in an apartment, just a kid, when his mother died. His elder brother was the bread-winner but he was on narcotics. An elderly Quaker couple raised Donald. He wasn't particularly bright, but S. accepted him and now he's working as a director of recreation in a slum area and doing excellent things."

Then there was the first Clinton boy who won a scholarship to a particular Ivy League university and decided that he didn't want to go there after all. "Boy, I really dressed him down," says Bernhard. "It was absolutely essential to place a good boy there to show them that Clinton could deliver the goods. He went. After that, we've been able to place two in some years, and one year three boys went there."

So the grapevine hums with activity. Messages in, messages out. The colleges, in their own interests, notify Clinton's advisory office of how students are shaping up. And in due course each boy gets a personal letter, which is really personal because he knows the advisors and they know him, either congratulating or commiserating, and offering suggestions and advice.

A monthly newsletter goes from Clinton to its college and university students. The files show the record of each of 800 colleges and universities in relation to Clinton diplomates, along with more opinionative records sent back by those students.

A university in the mid-west accepts in principle a student body recommendation that it admit thirty negro diplomates on lower averages. Not the sort of news item that makes headlines in New York, but a member of the student body has whipped off a note to Dr. Bernhard, and the name of a negro student has come out of Clinton's files and his application has been posted.

"But I never sold a shoddy kid," says Dr. Bernhard, with professional pride. "When I told one lad last year, with an average of 69, that he'd have to go three thousand miles and do Social Studies at a little religious college in K., I knew he'd succeed in K. Sure, I've sold a few risky kids, but I've always explained just what the risk was." So he tells, a trifle unhappily, of the brilliant young negro poet who was in perpetual rebellion against Clinton staff. Bernhard sent a selection of the lad's best work along with a truthful record to a prestige university, which gave him a full scholarship. When the poet was eventually expelled, nobody felt that he had been deceived.

"Some colleges call us up to recommend and report on boys," Bernhard adds. "They know that we know every boy, and that we see the long-term interests of our boys and of their institutions as being the same."

So, in the upshot, of Clinton's graduating class of 1000, well over half go to college, and ten per cent, which is the average for an academic school, win scholarships.

But is the school, necessarily, if not a soul-less diploma factory, nothing more than a somewhat soulful one?

In a vast establishment of 6000 students and 300 teachers, it would be impossible for the casual observer to pass a considered judgement. Discipline, I was assured, by people who were pretty clearly ready to reveal the seamy side of things to me, was very good. As in any school, a boy might "get fresh" with a teacher and find himself in trouble with authority, but the "blackboard jungle" picture was entirely inappropriate. In terms of good order, this is a good school; and so it seemed on my visits, with my notebooks carrying remarks about the very high level of student courtesy I met and observed, equal to that of the best schools I know.

There is a student self-government body that runs its own court, and sets many of its own rules, including the code of dress which was being passionately canvassed over the school's intercommunication system on one of the days when I was present. This student body has some rights of punishment (detention) and a teacher will normally report an offender to it rather than making his first complaint a major issue with the dean or assistant dean. There is a team of "squad boys" selected by the dean for a supervisory role over the buildings' 365,000 square feet and the (exceptionally large for New York) five acres of campus. As a final weapon, it is only for grave indiscipline, not for academic failure, that the law permits the school to exclude a student.

There is the typical U.S. Senior high school's wide range of co-curricular activities: 98 clubs, teams and squads catch up many of the boys in athletic and recreational programs. As usual, these activities are regarded as important for the intermeshing of personalities. But when I asked about integration I was told that it had only limited success. Superficially there were few racial problems, perhaps because there were no girls, from whose presence in other schools much of the inter-racial trouble seems to stem; but, in all the conditions (including overcrowding and overlapping of shifts) boys spend a limited total of out-of-class time on the campus, and prejudices bred in for a decade and a half are not easily eradicated.

Is Clinton a good school? It depends on what you can reasonably ask a school to do and to be accountable for. "In the last eleven years," said the assistant dean, "we've had ten boys who committed murders during their school years — not at school, of course; but that's ten out of 60,000, and the comparison is with the statistics for the sort of backgrounds they come from." Again, the potential problems of the regular truants are avoided rather than solved. And as in every educational situation in every school on the planet, more could always be done if limitless funds were available. Given Clinton's budget — about $800 per year per boy and equivalent to the national average — do you spend your marginal thousand dollars on trying to push a couple more borderline students into college, or on training a couple more of the below average to be competent assistant zoo-keepers, or on teaching two I.Q.-70 illiterates to read print? In writing a book of this nature, it is sometimes comforting to be able to pose such questions without having to supply the answers.

Is Clinton a good school? Given the limiting conditions and the set of the tide of events beyond its control, I have seen no school that achieves more.

14 All that money can buy?

Comprehensive School and Gymnasium. Sweden

Nothing could be more significant than the proportion of their resources that individuals and nations are prepared to devote to their various activities. If we find a wealthy nation or person spending vast sums on ever-increasing supplies of luxury consumer goods while failing to relieve the poverty of those desperately in need of even bare essentials. we can deduce — and criticize — a system of values inherent in this behaviour. If, of two nations approximately equal in wealth. one spends far more than the other on a higher quality and a greater quantity of freely provided education for its young people. it is a reasonable assumption that the bigger spender is relatively more concerned for the welfare of its future citizens.

The proposition may appear obvious enough, but unfortunately it is not. Too many factors still remain to be considered, and the chief of these is the question of what we are prepared to call "education." If. for example. a state found it economically worth while and technologically possible to keep young people at school until age 20 with little electrodes fitted into their brains through which, day in. day out, they could be uninterruptedly impregnated with high-level work skills (such as subserving computers), we would not necessarily see a heavy expenditure on this sort of program as evidence of a strong commitment to democratic human well-being. We should tend rather to interpret it as a form of investment in human capital by those controlling forces in the society who stood to benefit most (in their own estimation of benefit) from the dividends of such a policy. Again, if we found a nation claiming a vast increase in "educational" expenditure because it had made the simple book-keeping manoeuvre of transferring into that account either the costs of "educating" all its conscripts to be soldiers, sailors and airmen, or the cost of huge military and industrial research projects, we should have an uneasy feeling that the books had been cooked. Yet again, there would be much disagreement on the question of which of two equal spenders was doing the better educational job: one that divided its allocation of resources fairly equally amongst all its students, and one which discriminated heavily in favour of a particular group — elite or handicapped or underprivileged.

Now most of these things are already being done, or have been done in the past, except that instruction in work skills (which is only a narrow segment of the education of a human being) is still not into the electrode stage. Such instruction is, however, an increasingly intensive component in a process that some nations are pleased to call "education" even though, at some level of specialization or other, the term becomes an obvious misnomer.

Whether a human being is being "educated" is a subjective decision, depending on the values one proposes for his living, and the extent to which one believes that those values are being realized for him by what is happening in the schools and colleges and universities. Whether one nation is really devoting more resources of time and energy than another to "educating" its children is, therefore, ultimately a philosophic question, and not one that can be resolved by converting dollars to kronor and both to pesetas.

For what it is worth, Sweden is a country that spends — by reigning world standards — a very high proportion of its gross national product on schooling. The last time international comparisons were made (by UNESCO, in 1965) it ranked second in the world lists with 7.3%. Only Canada, with 8.5% of GNP, was higher, though Denmark and Norway and the U.S.S.R. were equal.

Sweden has geared her long-term educational plan (reaching into the 21st century) to her proposed specialist role as an automated society, a society in which, already, a score of highly skilled men produce a million superficial feet of timber from the day's quota of logs, while another small band of engineers, technologists and technicians turns an unending supply of trees into a mile of nineteen-feet-wide paper every three minutes.

Sweden would claim, also, to have one of the most egalitarian systems of education in the world. Its compulsory education is completely free, from the nation-wide generous proportion of teachers to students in every school, to the supply of every textbook and pencil to every child. As of 1970, at least 80% of students will enter some form of higher secondary education, and by 1980 that percentage will have risen to 95.

My main purpose in this chapter is to describe the magnificent material provision for education in Farsta, one of the largest schools in Stockholm; but in order to see Farsta clearly it is necessary to say a little about the context in which it is found.

By the end of the 1950's and the beginning of the 60's, the Swedes had made their plans for what they believe must be — in view of the inherence of continuous change in all foreseeable human activity — the last great overall re-shaping of education. They had opted for comprehensive* schooling to age 16, in the belief, for which broad research gave supporting though not con-clusive evidence, that little if anything would be lost in purely academic achievement, and that this little — if it existed at all — would be more than outweighed by compensatory gains in terms of character, social adjustment and social cohesion.

Compulsory schooling in Sweden begins at age 7 and con-tinues to age 16. The nine years are divided into three threes; lower, middle and high school. From age 16 the student follows one of three main streams of higher secondary education: **gym-nasium** (theoretical), leading eventually to university; **continua-tion school** (middle-job-oriented); or **vocational** (higher tech-nical). Within these main streams are a number of sub-streams.

In the 9th year of compulsory school the students of one class can choose amongst nine different sub-streams. In the five more theoretical streams, the optional subjects occupy seven of the 35 weekly periods and in the four streams with a practical bias the number is 22.

The Swedish Riksdag passed an act, however, in the autumn of 1968 about a reformed comprehensive school, that is to be introduced in 1971. The difference between the present and the new comprehensive school is above all that the 9th year will not be so clearly divided into sub-streams.

Farsta School has an enrolment of just over 1100 students, aged from 13 to 19, 700 of them at the senior comprehensive level, 400 at higher secondary. It is one of the largest schools in Stockholm, and it offers eight of the possible nine course options in ninth year. No other school offers so many.

Farsta was a product of the educational new deal that began at approximately the time the school was erected, in 1962. Planned in the stately manner, it stands, four-square and power-ful, off-white stone among the pure white of Sweden's winter snows.

"And what do you want next for your school, Mr. Lind-berg?" It was my near-final question as I sat facing the principal in his comfortable, executive-style office. He pondered the un-

---

* The term "comprehensive" is used here to differentiate from any system wherein children are selected for different schools on any grounds other than age or geography; the commonest such ground in the state systems of many countries is, of course, academic ability.

familiar English language and the import of my question for a second or two before responding. "At the moment, there is nothing. I am content."

It is an unusual, indeed an astounding answer for a school principal. But you could see Mr. Lindberg's point of view.

In the first and most vital place, his school was well staffed. He had 106 teachers, virtually all fully qualified, for his 1100 students. Of the 106, twenty-five worked approximately half-time, giving a staffing ratio of one full-time teacher to each 12 students.

Because of this generous supply of qualified teacher-power, Farsta had no problems of over-large classes. By law, the greatest possible number of students in any class in the Swedish nation is thirty (in the first three school years, twenty-five). But classes of this size may be halved for a variety of subjects — Swedish, foreign languages, laboratory work, craft. There is opportunity for teachers to be concerned with students as individuals rather than as masses.

In addition to teaching staff, Farsta, like all large Swedish schools, has the services of a psychologist, a doctor and a nurse. There is a minor army of non-professional staff — clerical workers, caretakers, janitors, laboratory assistants.

Space in the school is generous by any standard. Perhaps I should commence by describing classrooms, but I shall not. One index of the value a community places on education is the esteem in which it holds its teachers; and one reflection of this esteem is the conditions it affords them in their non-teaching time.

My visiting role in numerous schools makes me something of an expert on teachers' staff-rooms and I am "mentally set" to notice them. By and large they are far too small for their occupants: poky little cupboards for two, or large teacher-stables for thirty, furnished, so often, with old, dark-stained wooden tables and cheap, mass-produced pine bureaux that are piled with text-books and workbooks and essay papers. The bureau is the individual teacher's only office. The table is the communal lunch-area. And the corners of the room, forever creeping, glacier-like, towards the centre, are occupied by cooking facilities and sporting gear and teaching aids.

Not so in Farsta. The main staff area consisted of four contiguous rooms, rather more than three thousand square feet of air-conditioned space, built and furnished with all the quiet good taste and luxury of a highly successful architect's dream home.

Modern Scandinavian lounge chairs grouped round numerous polished timber tables. Charcoal and dark blue furnishings harmonizing with the off-white wallpaper, the high white ceilings, the white shaded table lamps, the huge, white-brick open fireplace. Carefully tended pot-plants in the windows. In the "quiet room" some hundreds of feet of wall space, lined with school-provided reference books and a couple of hundred current periodicals. Adjustable angle lamps at all the fifteen large study tables. A radio and a television set in one of the main staff rooms. Thoughtfully chosen pieces of sculpture in discreet nooks.

Coffee is taken here, between lessons, but not lunch. There is a teachers' section near the three vastly spacious and beautiful school dining rooms, all with their glowing timber walls and chairs, fawn drapes and tiled floors. Only one had a piano, but all three had large paintings — originals by recognized artists — on the end walls. The silent curriculum was at work in those rooms.

The music room, which also acts as an assembly hall, has seats — polished timber seats, of course — for 650, a full proscenium stage, Bechstein grand and a large concert organ. In the lofty, white ceiling are set some ninety house lights, and there are spotlights for theatrical performances.

And so on, and so on. For domestic science there are four large, modern kitchens, each equipped with four stoves, four double-sinks, four benches and tables, cupboards, refrigerator and freezer. Each of the two fully-furnished lounges has its piano. The classrooms are large (600 square feet), furnished with modern vari-height furniture. They are supplemented by "group rooms" designed to hold a maximum of sixteen students who are in split classes, or working on assignments, or tape recording poetry or foreign language work. (Farsta, though it has lost count of its many top-quality tape recorders, would like to have one for every room, along with the overhead projector, like Bredang School.) All the rooms are air-conditioned, beautifully decorated and furnished and splendidly equipped — looms in the textile room and expensive calculating machines — one to each two desks — in the commerce room, and in the woodwork area, masses of the precision equipment for which Sweden is famous.

All books and materials needed by all students are supplied free by the local authority, which meets approximately 40% of the running cost of the school, the State providing the rest. ("Somehow," said the head of another large Stockholm school, "we overspent on materials by 100,000 kronor (U.S. $20,000) last year. But of course there was no trouble: the authority found the money." I found, later, that next year's allowance was reduced to compensate.)

Up to the age of 16, Farsta's students receive no financial aid to study, but there is a child endowment payment of 75 kronor ($15 U.S.) per month made to the parents. For those at the upper secondary (gymnasium) levels, non-repayable allowances, subject to a means test, may go as high as $420 U.S. per year; for students over 21, additional, repayable, twenty-year student loans run to $1000 U.S. per year.

Like all Swedish teachers, Farsta's male and female staff receive equal pay within a progressive-taxation-and-social-benefits system that re-allocates a great deal of income from the family's second bread-winner (the married woman teacher without dependants) to provide security for the single-income family.

Has Farsta, then, all that money can buy? Do its students receive the best of all possible educations for the best of all possible worlds? I would have said not.

The nerve centre of any educational process is the point where students and teachers meet in human interaction. An education system can be worse than its teachers but it cannot possibly be better. If my children must be educated either by splendid teachers in a barn or by poor teachers in a palace, I shall choose the barn every time.

Neither Farsta nor the other Swedish schools I visited offers so stark a choice. The problem is not one of poor or hopeless teachers. But Sweden, like most countries, has not faced up to the problem, which is eventually an economic one, of providing full professional education as educators for all teachers. The average higher-comprehensive and gymnasium teacher — in Farsta and elsewhere — has completed a twelve-year course in the schools and a three-year academic course in the university. Older teachers have qualifications gained a long while ago, but a very recent development has been to add some professional training for all.

The result was that, in spite of splendid facilities and the small classes, I saw disappointingly little inspired or inspiring teaching. There was much work of a lecture-and-note-taking or lecture-interrupted-by-questioning nature, which would have been equally effective, one felt, with classes twice the size. Only once did I see signs of real learner-oriented rather than teacher-dominated work. Farsta has plenty of good, solid, average teachers doing good, solid, average work. But excitement and joy did not appear dominant.

In common with buildings of other "new wave" schools, those at Farsta, about which I have so far been so enthusiastic, are indeed of splendid quality and décor, but they are lacking in flexibility. They are solid single-class (or half-class) rooms, with the usual additions of science complexes (laboratory-plus-class-room). Should Farsta ever want to change to a different learning pattern — say, lecture-and-tutorial which requires a number of large rooms and a great many group-rooms — a lot of architectural ingenuity will be needed in subdividing some class-rooms and removing load-bearing walls between others.

All in all, one would say that what money has so far bought Farsta is what most educationists would have regarded as a really splendid education in the early 1950's.

Behind and beneath the situation is the perpetual dilemma of the welfare state: what to do when one has achieved welfare. I am a fierce proponent of the welfare state, which is merely a social attempt to ensure for all citizens the same freedom from deprivation through poverty and sickness that the most ardent opponents of such a state habitually confer on their own families as soon as they are economically able.

Yet the problem remains. Between the lowest-paid and the highest-paid teacher in Farsta the salary differs by only 25% of the latter's, and steeply progressive taxation eats up a lot of the difference anyway. It is generally agreed that, economically, it isn't worth anybody's while to be a principal: the extra income does not nearly compensate for the extra duties.

If the economic incentive is removed, another must take its place. I suggest that it should be a divine dissatisfaction akin to the artist's; and this is the sort of motivation that flows from an awareness — in turn the outcome, for most people, of broad, deep and inspiring preparation — of the endless vista of potential human development that the best education can provide. Without this, the job is just another job. Administrators told me, sincerely, that daring innovation was welcomed and encouraged. Teachers assured me, with equal sincerity, that Sweden was not the place to look for daringly innovative schools. The statements are compatible. To be free to innovate, in education or violin-playing, all but the rare genius need trained insight as well as encouragement.

I thought I detected something of the same Western malaise in the students, something perilously close to conformism without a cause. Everybody is going to succeed and competition is frowned on. "It is unfair to set much homework," a teacher told me. "Some children have better facilities and assistance at home than others." And if education, however egalitarian, is patterned to the achievement of economic goals **that, in effect, have already been achieved,** where then is the incentive? Should the new goal for youth lie in new possibilities of self-realization in creative pursuits, rather than an equal opportunity to earn another 6000 kronor a year? Or should it have a more international, humane shape? Or can it combine both?

I suspect that, in Farsta as throughout Sweden, youth still seeks an answer.

15 The nest or the cage

Tagore's School at Santinitekan. India

"The image of the Western school is a cage. My school shall be a nest." Thus spake Rabindra Nath Tagore of the school that has become Visva-Bharati, meeting-place for the learning of East and West, **yatra visvam bhavatyekanidam** "where the world makes its home in a single nest".

"Civilised man has come far away from the orbit of his normal life. He has gradually formed and intensified some habits, that are like those of the bees, for adapting himself to his hive-world. We so often see modern men suffering from ennui, from world-weariness, from a spirit of rebellion against their environment for no reasonable cause whatever. Social revolutions are constantly ushered in with a suicidal violence that has its origin in our dissatisfaction with our hive-wall arrangement — the too exclusive enclosure that deprives us of the perspective which is so much needed to give us the proper proportion in our art of living. . . .

"In our highly complex modern condition, mechanical forces are organized with such efficiency that the materials produced grow far in advance of man's selective and assimilative capacity to simplify them into harmony with his nature and needs. Such an intemperate over growth of things, like the rank vegetation of the tropics, creates confinement for man. The nest is simple, it has an easy relationship with the sky; the cage is complex and costly, it is too much itself, excommunicating whatever lies outside. And modern man is busy building his cage, fast developing his parasitism on the monster, THING, whom he allows to envelop him on all sides. He is always occupied in adapting himself to its dead angularities, limits himself to its limitations, and merely becomes a part of it."

I take from its shelf a volume of educational and philosophic thought. Plato, Aristotle, Aquinas . . . Comenius, Locke, Rousseau, Dewey . . . intellectual giants who have set their seal on the culture and the schools of the West.

Intellectual giants.   And Tagore breathes the same philosophic air of the heights they dominate.

Yet which Western philosopher in two thousand years has been also poet, dramatist and composer, even in a humble way? Bertrand Russell, brilliant, fluent and copious, has published eighty books in mathematical and philosophical and related fields. Tagore (who died in 1941) published almost two hundred books, of which a hundred are in verse, half-a-hundred are dramatic works, the rest shared amongst philosophy and fiction.   In a land of song he composed two thousand songs that are still sung.   In a culture where dance is universal and an integral part of religion he created a new form of dance that survives his death.

Western education has followed the path of the intellect, the path of Plato, Dewey and the rest.   For Tagore, intellect is one vital component in Man's total being; but other aspects of his nature are also vital; no society dare neglect and no school should neglect these other aspects to concentrate too single-mindedly and narrow-mindedly on the conscious reason.

"Through this great deficiency of our modern education, we are condemned to carry to the end a dead load of dumb wisdom.   Like miserable outcasts, we are deprived of our place in the festival of culture, and wait at the outer court, where the colours are not for us, nor the forms of delight, nor the songs.   Ours is the education of a prison-house, with hard labour and with a drab dress cut to the limits of minimum decency and necessity.   We are made to forget that the perfection of colour and form and expression belongs to the perfection of vitality — that the joy of life is only the other side of the strength of life.   The timber merchant may think that the flowers and foliage are mere frivolous decorations of a tree; but if these are suppressed, he will know to his cost that the timber too will fail."

The name Visva-Bharati belongs to the University — co-educational, residential, with its students drawn from all over India and overseas and with visiting university teachers constantly in residence.   But the huge campus (11.4 square miles) accommodates, and Visva-Bharati unites, schools and colleges for children, adolescents, and adults from the age of six upwards.

How do you create a school that shall be a nest rather than a cage?   At Santiniketan, 150 kilometres north of Calcutta, Tagore, then forty years of age, founded his school.   It was to be a place for full, rich living rather than for the deadly grinding at facts that characterized the transplanted British school in Indian soil. Above all, it was to be a school open to nature.

Santiniketan began with a small group of orphans and destitute boys who learned not only reading and writing but art and music and nature study, who grew vegetables and who chopped wood, wove cloth and improved their buildings and, above all, learned an attitude to life and each other that erased the boundary line between work and play.

"For these boys," wrote Tagore, "vocation has no meaning. Their studies, though strenuous, are not a task, being permeated by a holiday spirit . . . It is because their class-work has not been wrenched away and walled in from their normal vocation, because it has been made a part of their daily current of life, that it easily carries itself by its own flow."

Today at Santiniketan primary and secondary school classes are held beneath the straight, tall **sal** trees, in the mango groves and the **amloki** groves. Each student carries a small piece of carpet to sit on. Low circular concrete benches can serve as tables or seats. There is a small raised seat for the teacher. For each lesson, the class changes to another location.

I have letters and essays from students whom I met in Santiniketan, in which they describe their outdoor school life. The English sometimes frames itself in a manner that is forced or stilted or a trifle out of idiom, yet the ring of truth is there:

"The rainy season goes away. The autumn enters. My eyes sink in the green paddy fields. The earth beams with radiance. The clear blue sky with some white boat-like sailing clouds stares at us. Our minds are also radiant with happiness."

"The nature study classes are held in the fields and woods. Boys climb on the trees to find caterpillars. The children can name each bird by hearing its sound."

"During the blazing summer we feel miserable, yet one gets a wonderful feeling to have the classes under the trees and watch the thirsty birds screaming from their branches."

"We have come over the disadvantages because of open air education system, rapidly, easily and actively. We have also made ourselves accustomed to the visitors and their noises around the school campus. Their negotiations (? conversations) and the songs of birds from tree tops are all the same to us."

Behind the idea of a school where the atmosphere counts for as much as the subject matter, where contentment and joy and harmony with the world of sun and breeze and sky and living things rank higher than success in trigonometry and grammar and physics — behind all this lay the frustration of so much that was fully and deeply and truly human in the child Tagore.

"The founding of my school had its origin in the memory

of that longing for freedom, the memory which seems to go back beyond the sky-line of my birth.

Freedom in the mere sense of independence has no content, and therefore no meaning. Perfect freedom lies in the perfect harmony of relationship which we realize in this world — not through our response to it in **knowing,** but in **being.** Objects of knowledge maintain an infinite distance from us who are the knowers. For knowledge is not union. Therefore the farther world of freedom awaits us there where we reach truth, not through feeling it by our senses, or knowing it by reason but through the union of perfect sympathy.

Children with the freshness of their senses come directly to the intimacy of this world. This is the first great gift they have. They must accept it naked and simple and must never again lose their power of immediate communication with it. For our perfection we have to be vitally savage and mentally civilized; we should have the gift to be natural with nature and human society."

"In the usual course I was sent to school, but possibly my suffering was unusual, greater than that of most other children. The non-civilized in me was sensitive; it had the great thirst for colour, for music, for movement of life. Our city-built education took no heed of that living fact. It had its luggage-van waiting for branded bales of marketable results. The relative proportion of the non-civilized and civilized in man should be in the proportion of water and land on our globe, the former predominating."

Most Santineketan students are in residence. Fees are relatively high — a hundred rupees a month in Bengal where twice that sum is the salary of an experienced high-school teacher. Unhappily, such exclusiveness seems inescapable. Nowhere in the world do I know of a school in which a daring innovator can be free of government control and which can rid itself completely of the inevitable restriction of entry to those who can afford it.

A school day at Santineketan is a long one, if you measure it by the standards of the normal school. A bell rings ("merrily from the large tower" says one of my student correspondents) as early as 4.30 a.m. in summer. By 6.15 (7 to 7.30 in cooler seasons) the students and staff are washed, dressed, breakfasted, have tidied their rooms and are ranged in order outside the library for **vaitalik,** morning prayer assembly. A hymn from the Upanishad is followed by a song of Tagore — **gurudeva,** divine teacher. Then all go outside to morning lessons, five periods (with a break after the second).

"After those five periods we do not feel tired because our education is not a weight put on our head but we are taught in a fine and simple way."

For the long lunch time of two or two-and-a-half hours, the day scholars return to their nearby homes and the boarders move to the general kitchen-dining-room. Afternoon classes for two hours or so covering practical activities — laboratory work, art and craft — frequently move into the classroom.

Teaching method relies a good deal on conversation and discussion, the initiative lying with students as well as teachers. Setting, atmosphere and method go back to ancient Indian and Greek procedure.

"Our teachers," says a student, "are not merely teachers for different subjects, but they are our whole-time companions and guides . . . they are like our brothers and sisters." And another: "The teacher . . . comes with a cheerful mind . . . The teachers are ready answering all sorts of questions. They do not laugh at our foolish questions . . ."

After classes, there are various forms of physical education, a compulsory part of the curriculum. Then the students gather for a brief evening meditation, following which the day scholars return to their homes and the boarders to their hostels. In the evening there are supervised periods of private study and evening prayers before bedtime.

Tuesday is the evening of the **sahitya sabha,** the literary meeting. The program is arranged by a student committee, and consists of readings of students' own essays and poems, singing and dancing (sometimes in national dress).

"Mind, when long deprived of its natural food of truth and freedom of growth, develops an unnatural craving for success; and our students* have fallen victims to the mania for success in examinations. Success consists in obtaining the largest number of marks with the strictest economy of knowledge. It is a deliberate cultivation of disloyalty to truth, of intellectual dishonesty, of a foolish imposition by which the mind is encouraged to rob itself. But as we are by means of it made to forget the existence of mind, we are supremely happy at the result. We pass examinations, and shrivel up into clerks, lawyers and police inspectors, and we die young."

Wednesday is Santiniketan's weekly holiday, chosen because the **asram** (the school and campus) was founded on that day. There is a minor shock in what follows as illustration of the second sentence of this passage from a senior student's writing:

"Unlike every other school we have our weekly holiday on Wednesday instead of Sunday. The boys and girls make full use of this holiday. Early in the morning we go to the **mendir** (prayer hall) where we sing a few devotional songs

* Tagore is speaking here of India's students, not Santiniketan's.   H.P.S.

and then say our prayers. Then a group of boys and girls go from door to door asking for help for the poor. All these things are collected together and once a month or twice a month they go to the villages and offer money and clothes to the villagers." Others, the writer adds, spend their holiday cleaning litter and fallen leaves from the **asram.**

Inevitably, in a school that is a nest, the seasons are extremely important. In the monsoon season, many more classes take place indoors. Other classes become nature walks to study the countryside and the erosion of the **khvais** (small canyons).

"Sometimes in a rainy day we have an outing to some nearby places. We walk there singing and smell the fresh air of villages and rivers."

And the seasonal festivals and functions are observed. Says Rabindranath, "When the kiss of rain thrilled the hearts of surrounding trees, if we had still behaved with propriety and paid all our attention to mathematics it would have been positively wrong, impious."

Varsha-Mangal, Festival of Rains is in July and August, and in early August there fall the Tree-planting Festival and the Ploughing Ceremony. There are the Autumn Festival and the Spring Festival, as well as a number of anniversaries — New Year, Rabindranath's Birthday and Death Anniversary and so on — and a Crafts Festival.

This is a book about schools and children; but Visva-Bharati is an organic whole. Its Higher Secondary School (to age 17) offers what looks rather like a standard Western high-school course except that it includes Indian Languages, ethics and psychology, and an unusually wide range of aesthetic subjects: vocal music, instrumental music, drawing, painting and modelling. Work here leads to a College of under-graduate and Graduate Studies, offering a B.Sc. and a B.A.

Above this again is a College of Postgraduate Studies and Research, conceived as a meeting-place of the many Indian sub-cultures and the cultures of both East and West. Here scholars from all corners of the earth visit to lecture in and to discuss language and literature, history and philosophy.

There is a College of Fine Art and Crafts, offering certificate and diploma courses. A College of Music and Dance gives a post-matriculation four-year diploma, with students specializing in different kinds of music or dancing. The College of Teaching produces specialist teachers for arts, craft and music as well as for basic training and primary and secondary education.

From Santiniketan you walk (or drive) a mile to Sriniketan. The campus terrain is flat and green. "This is our land," says your guide, "but over there the land belongs to the village." There is no fence or dividing line, and this is as it should be, for Sriniketan seeks to identify itself as closely as possible with the neighbouring community.

Siksha-Satra, once established at Santiniketan, is a multipurpose type of higher secondary school with different courses that include humanities, science, technical, woodcraft and home science. Siksha-charcha was established as an institute to train rural teachers. Loka Siksha Samshad encourages basic study in the homes for those who lack formal education, and reaches out into 70 centres.

Then there is Silpa-Sadana, the Cottage Industry Training Centre, a centre for crafts, that issues diplomas and certificates and runs one-year courses, bringing into its scope weaving, woodwork, basketry, leatherwork, pottery, toymaking, lacquerwork and electrical and mechanical training. At one level the diplomates now produce distinctive and lovely Sriniketan silkwork, like the tissue-fine red-brown-and-gold scarf with bird-and-twigs motif that I brought away with me. The electrical and mechanical apprentices become a semi-skilled labour group. And much of Cottage Industry is just that: the use of simple skills of handicraft by peasant women in their homes.

As the villages come to Sriniketan, so Sriniketan goes to the villages. Visva-Bharati's Department of Rural Reconstruction runs an agricultural farm, a dairy and a poultry farm, the results of whose experimental work reach out to two hundred villages in the form of improved methods of farming and soil conservation, better strains of seed and cuttings, breeding cocks, chicks and eggs, and the loan of high-quality bulls.

And so on, and so on. From the great complex that is Visva-Bharati stem health centres and maternity centres, youth clubs and library services, a Village Boy Scout Movement, anti-malarial and leprosy control units; all directed to enlightening the ignorance and thereby alleviating the poverty and the suffering that are the age-old lot of village India.

To squalor, sickness, pain and ignorance the eye and heart and voice of Tagore responded with the vision and sympathy and immediacy of the great humane artist.

"We must so endeavour that a power from within the villages may be working alongside of us, albeit undiscernible by us . . . If I can free only one or two villages from the bonds of ignorance and weakness, there will be built, on a tiny scale, an ideal for the whole of India . . . Our aim must be to give these villagers complete freedom, education for all, the winds of joy blowing across the village, music and recitation going on, as in the old days. Fulfil this ideal in a few villages only, and I will say that these few villages are my India. And only if that is done, will India be truly ours."

16 One world at school

The International School. Geneva, Switzerland

In 1968 internationalism stood about where Christianity did 1600 years earlier: a weakling faith, dubiously viable, yet offering the brightest ray of hope to mankind in a dark world.

I should think that any extra-terrestrial Intelligence looking at our planet through some cosmic telescope would have decided, when the first atomic bomb exploded in 1945, that the only hope of survival for mankind lay in the education of its members to an international outlook.   Developments since then have added more and different evidence without altering the conclusion. And many dedicated minds and hearts have been at work in the cause both before and after the first A-day.

The International School of Geneva opened in October 1924 with four teachers and eight students. Today it has 1540 students and 130 teachers, though the increase is due rather to the growth of official business between nations than to a massive increase in commitment to internationalist ideals.

Children of sixty-two nations and one stateless child (the truest internationalist, perhaps?) attend the International School. Rather more than 48% (675) of all those enrolled are from the U.S.A.   The next largest contingent of 183 (13%) come from the United Kingdom, and along with 8 Canadians*, a handful of Australians and a few New Zealanders the "Anglo-Saxons" make up just on two out of three of the student body.

The parents are a group such as one might expect in a fee-paying school in Geneva: 45% are in the fields of Industry, Commerce and Banking, another 10% in the learned professions, and 25% are with intergovernmental organizations, U.N. and specialized bodies.   Most of the rest are in diplomatic, consular or military service, or employed by the school itself, international

---

* There are also ten French-speaking Canadians.

church bodies and the like.

Until last year, the school was organized in two main sections: a large (1109) English-language section and a smaller (340-plus) French-language section. From September 1968, the two sections have been partly integrated with blocked time-tables in languages, Physical Education, Art, Music and School activities. Most, but not all children study, if this is possible, in the section that speaks their native language as its first tongue, though a small but significant minority cross the linguistic border for the early primary years.

In any case, bilinguilism is one of the more obvious aspects of the school's avowedly internationalist policy. In the English section, conversational French is begun in the earliest nursery class and definite teaching in Grade 1; in the French section the commencement of English is delayed until Grade 2 level.

Although language is only the machinery of international understanding and speakers of the same tongue have massacred each other throughout all centuries including our own, it is a tremendously important piece of machinery nevertheless. I have communicated basic humour in pantomime in a few countries where students and I had no interpreter and no common language and we knew we were friends; but in classroom after classroom I could establish rapport more or less in proportion to the group's mastery of English. In Singapore, with a roomful of reasonably fluent fifteen-year-olds, I enjoyed a gay discussion comparing our two countries. Two days later in Bangkok I talked a little with a teacher in his halting English and tried, but with little success, to get through him to his class to find out how they thought and felt.

In Geneva, at Ecolint (école internationale) the students told me the same story: friendship could cross the national barrier more readily than the linguistic one. A Pakistani boy and a Texas boy could and did become friends if both spoke English; so could a Japanese and a Swiss girl, if both spoke French; (the girls, I am told, are much more flexibly open to the influence of a heterogeneous community); even an Israeli and an Egyptian student with a language bridge between them could get along; but without it, how could two human beings find many common interests to share?

This is a key problem, then, only partway solved even in Ecolint. The gifted minority gain most from encountering the two national cultures. The many develop their bilingualism at the neighbourhood and friendship levels, but not to the point of having a fluent, facile instrument functioning well enough for difficult study; and the unconscious cultural and philosophic assumptions structured into language go very deep indeed.

Peter Quince once reported in a British journal **The Teacher** how seven conference members from six nations sat down to produce a routine questionnaire, simply to obtain discussion material for a future assembly. The subject was agreed upon, only the details had to be concluded. The seven committee members were skilled in reconciling viewpoints, had no axes to grind; they were reasonable people, anxious for agreement, and they had abundant facilities for translation. But the patterns of thought were so different that after two hours of discussion not one question on the questionnaire had been agreed on.

The fact that language skills are not perfect is not a total barrier to agreement. Part of the harmonizing process comes through curriculum. A history or a geography lesson in any culture takes on new dimensions when children from other cultures that are involved in the material being studied are able to show how differently things sometimes look through other spectacles. This is particularly true of current events where national interests are at stake. It is not simply a matter of people learning to understand and be nice to each other, though that is part of what happens. It is also, and simultaneously, an enrichment of each student's insight into the world.

Even more is that true in art, where children from all the continents draw and paint and sculpt in a way that emphasizes both cultural differences and human affinities. In Indian, Chinese and Japanese art, for example, form has retained a highly important place, whereas Western art, during the nineteenth century, began to emphasize line and subject matter.

Children's free work reflects such cultural differences. In a subject where there is not the same demand for convergence on a body of knowledge as in mathematics and science, the greater difficulty and vital aim is to preserve individuality of approach. Fortunately there are neither text-books nor a set syllabus to exert pressure towards a homogenizing process. Students silently educate each other through art, at first below the level of consciousness, later at higher levels.

What matters, however, is not the subject but the spirit in which it is taught. Thus a science teacher explained to me enthusiastically how excellent a vehicle science teaching can be for fostering internationalism. No subject is more universal in its application, and examples drawn from round the world tellingly make the point.

Teachers of sixteen nationalities add variety to presentation of work. In January 1968, of 112 full-time teachers, sixty were from the United Kingdom, nineteen from Switzerland, twelve were French. For some, a post at the International School is simply another teaching position, fairly well paid, in a pleasant and interesting cosmopolitan city. For others it is all this and also, sometimes above all else, an opportunity to work towards world unity. By and large, however, they are a well travelled group. Staff friendships transcend national barriers. Frequently, too, staff members are married to members of another nation, example educating better than precept.

Internationalism, said one teacher, is not merely taught but lived. The student council and the student-organized sporting and social clubs are international, with multi-national officials. There is, of course, correspondence between students of the school and those of schools in the homelands of some class member. There are experiments in time-tabling to allow of interchange of staff and senior students between the English-speaking and French-speaking sections. The great Greek amphitheatre is the only assembly "hall". It is a splendid one, in a magnificent setting and was the work of staff and student hands from the four corners of the earth. And in this kind of community, journeys to neighbouring and distant countries, with all the educational benefits to language, the social studies and human insights are a matter of course. Deliberately, class groups are created that mix the nationalities and, other things being equal, a class with a preponderance of U.S. students will be taken by a U.K. teacher and vice versa, rather than keeping the teacher with more of his own nationals.

In a Geneva school community, current international events loom large. There is a Student United Nations, again student-organized, a voluntary co-curricular body. It is allowed to use the Palais des Nations for its debates, which follow the U.N. activities. Issues from colonialism to border disputes and arms sale and hunger are taken up, projects are developed, and the participants do not need to feign interest.

Ask any teacher in any country the three main barriers to better education and he will list them for you: lack of money; parents; examinations.

Lack of money has confined Ecolint to premises more romantic in appearance than functional in pedagogy. It has also imposed the world-wide upper-class pattern of private fee-paying schools. In 1968 the school was formally altered from an Association to a Foundation, one object being to attract massive finance for the granting of scholarships — the number 500 is mentioned hopefully.

Children in the International School atmosphere not unnaturally will often develop more international, that is, less nationalistic sentiments than those of their parents; indeed, if none did so, the avowed primary objective of the school would be called into question. This situation sometimes leads to strong differences of opinion with those parents who see the school as a convenient and linguistically versatile instructional centre in a foreign city rather than as the nurturing ground of a new supra-national ideology.

Money can be raised, sometimes, and parents can be overcome by determined offspring, always; but examinations are the very devil. They flout the international school not only in the usual national ways, but in other and more complex ones as well.

For obvious reasons, most parents — and the students too for the matter of that — are anxious that the period of international high school shall be followed by a tertiary education in the home country from which they are temporary, though sometimes long-term, exiles.

This is natural and reasonable enough, but the resulting problems are manifold. French universities traditionally demand a formidable mastery of the more abstruse disciplines;* English "A" level examinations which are used as a matriculation sieve, though they are not in toto as intense as their French equivalents, are very different in their narrow-range specialization from the broader, more varied and flexible College Entrance examinations that precede admission to tertiary education in the U.S. In practice, it is simply not possible to prepare students for these final high-school examinations if they remain in the same classes.

From Ecolint, therefore, came the move for an international baccalaureat (or matriculation) that should be an admission qualification acceptable in as many countries as possible. There is now an International Baccalaureat Office experimenting gingerly with 500 students in Ecolint and other international schools. In the early stages, and it is a question of years before even the early stages are completed, it is becoming evident that not even all major countries can be brought into the plan. The millenium is some way off.

So the work goes on. Comparative religion in the history syllabus, philosophy in the twelfth grade, music as another cross-cultural link. There is no subject in the curriculum that cannot be treated internationally, if doing so seems sufficiently important to those participating.

"Do you really learn to think more internationally here?" I asked some of the senior boys. "Well, yes," they agreed cautiously — at least they learned to understand people of other nations more, even if not always to agree with them. A narrow base, perhaps, on which to build the future of a planet. But aside from it — what?

---

* So do Swiss ones, which is one reason why so few local children attend Ecolint.